Haunted Estill County

Tales of Ghosts, Legends, & Mysterious Events

Copyright © 2013 by Rebecca Patrick-Howard

www.rebeccaphoward.net

Published by Mistletoe Press

All rights reserved. No part of this book may be reproduced, scanned, or distributed in any printed or electronic form without permission.

First Edition: April 2013

Printed in the United States of America

For Jim, who loved a good ghost story

Table of Contents

Introduction 1

Hoof Beats in the Mist 6

Isolation in the Woods 14

Irvine: A Hotbed for UFO Activity? 21

The Music Never Stopped 34

On the Line 40

The Ghost of the Headless Timberman 44

The Case of the Mysterious Government Agent ... 46

South Irvine Tragedy 52

An Accidental Murder 56

The Ghostly Passenger 59

Myth or Truth? 62

The Shadow People 66

The Haunting of Barnes Mountain 79

The Devil's House 89

Dark Hollow Road	98
The Black Dog of Death	103
A Haunting in Pryse	111
The Oil Boom Murders	115
Restless Spirits	120
Trotting Ridge Cemetery	128
The Big Cats	131
The Drowning Creek Ambush	134
Gabriel's Trumpet	139
Unsolved Murders	144
The Daisy Horn Case	145
Farcilla (Fairalie) Reece	148
The Dave Woolery Case	152
The Bear Horn Case	156
Loretta Willoughby	159
Alex Richardson	161
The Furnaces	164
Bumps in the Night	168
The Bells of South Irvine	174
Folk Superstitions	177
Acknowledgements	183
References	186

River houses in Ravenna

Haunted Estill County

Introduction

I am a huge fan of ghost stories. When I was younger I wanted to grow up to be a parapsychologist. (Well, either that or a cowgirl depending on which day of the week you asked me!) I wasn't exactly sure what the word meant, but I heard it on TV and it sounded like someone who got to chase ghosts and that sounded fabulous to me at the time. I was eight, after all. I loved listening to my family members tell ghost stories and

Haunted Estill County

some of my favorite movies were films featuring haunted houses and restless spirits.

Ghost stories are still important to me and over the years I have collected many. Tall tales, urban legends, paranormal encounters, folk stories, cryptology–I love them all. I love the chill factor and the history behind the stories and I am especially interested in stories that don't seem to change much from person to person, even if the people themselves have never met one another.

Although there are a few different paranormal books written about various parts of the state, I wanted to create a book solely based on paranormal experiences and folktales from Estill County. I think as you keep reading you'll find there are quite a few of them, too! I have tried not to focus so much on the clanging and clattering and things that go "bump" in the night. Instead, I was interested in some of the back stories of the hauntings which are often scarier than the ghosts themselves.

Unless the stories have a historical basis, none of the following tales have any solid "proof" to them–at least not any shown to me. That is my disclaimer. You might read about a certain area and wonder why you've never heard that particular tale before. I can't answer that. I can honestly say, however, all of the following stories were told to me by people who live in Estill County. Some might be true and some might be tall tales, but I think they're all pretty fun and interesting.

People often wonder why one person who lives in a place, or visits it, might have a ghostly encounter when another person won't have one at all. Some people believe it takes a catalyst in order for a paranormal experience to occur. You don't have to be psychic to encourage the experiences, but you might be sensitive in a way that makes opening the doorway just a little bit easier. That's why some people might be able to live in a house without ever hearing a single unexplained noise while someone else might not be able to stay more than a night. This is just one theory, of course.

Unless the site I am talking about in the following pages is a public one I have refrained from using house numbers and street names. Almost all of the houses in these stories are currently inhabited, unless otherwise noted. I didn't think the owners and/or renters would like a bunch of us driving by in the middle of the night, trying to catch a spook in action.

When it was possible, I did visit the locations I have written about. And, yes, in more than one place I certainly felt some tingles and unexplained chills. I do believe many of the locations in this book might truly have something a little extra special about them.

Haunted Estill County

Estill County is indeed a fascinating place, filled with creepy tales and old stories. During my late night writing sessions I often found myself looking over my shoulder and making sure my doors were locked. I hope you find these as fun and spooky as I did!

Haunted Estill County

Hoof Beats in the Mist

There are many hollows and valleys in Estill County and some of them are so hidden by the mountains that their entrances are nigh on unknown and unseen by strangers to the area. It's easy to laugh about the fact that one side of the county often has no idea what goes on when it comes to the other side–even when it concerns the weather.

Haunted Estill County

It can be an overwhelmingly beautiful experience to drive through the mountains and the back roads and hollows in the spring when the leaves are budding on the trees and the sparsely decorated hillsides of winter become alive and awakened again in the pleasant temperatures of April and May. The rich valley floors are host to fertile pastures and winding creeks creeping past stalwart barns and farms that have, in some cases, been in families for generations.

At night, however, the feel of the valley can change. Darkness creeps in faster in these nooks and crannies of the mountains and the height of the trees and the hills can block out the sunlight before it fades away in town and on tops of the windy ridges. And on those nights when the air is just right and the fog starts sliding in along the valley floor, it can become a different place indeed.

One of the most beautiful valleys in the county is close to the Lee County line. Here, at the foot of a large, towering mountain with a winding road that leads up onto a ridge that seems to touch the sky, is a large farmhouse. Unlike many that have been abandoned and forgotten over the years, this farmhouse is still standing tall and proud and boasts white paint, a solid porch, and outbuildings that have been well taken care of. Its position is an awkward one, located in a triangle created by mountain and road, but it stands alone with no other houses around it. Like a sentry, it guards the road that weaves behind it and disappears into the trees. It's not an easy house to get to, yet everyone must drive past it to access the ridge where so many make their homes.

If there ever was a history to the house, and there must be considering its age, then it's been forgotten by most in the area. Who lived in it, what they did, and where they are now are not stories circulating through the valley anymore. It's a relic of times gone by, its imposing beauty not marked by age but exemplified by it. The valley beyond has been written about extensively; it's full of stories and legends of its once boisterous industry and township which no longer exist. This particular house, however, is a mystery. It sets alone, forgotten, except by those who drive by it and wonder about what might go on inside.

It is not without its own stories, however, when it comes to the supernatural. Those who have ventured close to it on just the right night have come away with stories defying logic.

Although there are no large animals kept nearby, when the fog is thick and the air is still, the sounds of trumpeting hoof beats can be heard echoing throughout the grounds. The noise begins softly at first, a mere whisper that could be explained as the rattle of an approaching car as it speeds down the mountainside around the house. When no headlights emerge through the dense fog that has slowly snaked its way across the grass and creek and has slid up over the barn and porches, then the sound might be mistaken for a family of deer, for surely the mountains are full of them. The hoof beats are more powerful than those the spindly deer can make, though, and there are many of them, far more than a simple family of three or four could produce. If you were to stand close to the house you might swear they were coming at you from all directions, filling the air with their clomps and scratches, making the very ground beneath you shudder in their wake. You might even try to run for cover, convinced a team of horses would break through the wall of whiteness within seconds and thunder upon you.

But no team of horses has ever been spotted.

Although the noise is loud enough to feel deep inside the soul, there are no carriages or angry riders that fly across the fields–at least not any earthly ones. If you do manage to stand there long enough, however, and wait then you might see the fog part for just a second. And, if you do, then you might notice a lone white horse with a brilliant, shimmering mane and a coat that gleams in the moonlight. While the property boasts no large farm animals, and surely this beautiful creature would fade away as quickly as he came if you tried to touch him, he is there when the fog comes in. Is he protecting those from the other hoof beats? Is there something more sinister going on at the foot of the mountain and the horse a guard that keeps the evil at bay? Not all spirits take the form of humans.

In fact, there might even be another animal spirit that haunts the area. As well as the horse, a phantom goat has been seen around the property, too. This dark and menacing creature with its sharp horns and steely glare feels out of place to those who have seen it and, when faced with the vision of the horse, quickly disappears into the fog.

More than one person has visited this residence and spoken of seeing a "ghostly white horse" that disappears after several seconds of looking at it. Others have heard the sounds of hoof beats when the fog is thick around the property, almost blotting out the outside world.

Haunted Estill County

Isolation in the Woods

Note: I have collected many Estill County ghost stories. It's sometimes uncanny the way several different people who have no knowledge of one another will tell a similar story about the same place. The following is a story given to me by someone who lives in the county. They shall remain anonymous, and the storyteller will know I have expanded on her original story, but the story itself is a true one and the following events really happened to the best of my knowledge right here in Estill County.

Haunted Estill County

Not all ghost stories can be explained by the passing of a loved one. Some popular television shows will try to convince viewers that the things going bump in the night are demons, angels, or possessions–or even a combination of the three. Of course, there is always the ever popular "Indian burial ground" narrative that has been the backbone for many ghost stories, especially since the popularity of the "Poltergeist" franchise in the mid 1980s. Sometimes, though, the reason behind the haunting is almost as scary as the haunting itself.

Despite its close proximity to Richmond, Winchester, Lexington, and the Mountain Parkway (the long stretch of rural highway connecting most of our isolated eastern counties) Estill County remains somewhat veiled. You don't have to drive but a minute or two off of Main Street before you're in the mountains. In fact, despite the fact that HWY 52 is flat

Haunted Estill County

and three lanes in parts of Madison County, as it snakes up around Tipton Ridge in Estill you could almost meet yourself coming around some of those curves, leading you to suspect it's not really a major road at all but that you somehow wandered off of it. It's easy to believe there are places in this county nobody has ever been to. There are roads here that defy Mapquest and modern GPS systems. A person could really get lost if they wanted to and many people do.

Several years ago, Mrs. Susan Walters and her husband moved into one of the most isolated parts of the county. Their home was a retreat in the thick woods, down a road the county claimed to maintain but was still rough around the edges. It was little more than a logging road. Indeed, she and her husband put the gravel in themselves for the last fifty feet of it so they could get the trucks in to move their furniture.

Not long after they moved their last load in and began unpacking, the singing started. Oftentimes it

Haunted Estill County

would be the faint sounds of a woman singing a soothing lullaby; easily passed off as the wind through the trees, the sounds of neighbors on down the mountain with a radio echoing off the cliffs, or even a slight trick of the imagination–in the beginning, anyway. As these things will do, however, the singing was soon too distinct to be confused with anything other than what it was. Mrs. Walters knew the sound herself for even as adults there are some things from childhood that feel as close today as they ever did. It was a lullaby if she had ever heard one and it was a mother's voice singing it.

While the soft singing was eerie, it was beautiful in its own way and there was clearly no harm in it so the Walters let it pass. Soon, it became part of the house. It wasn't long, however, until the sounds of animals running across the floor at night became a common occurrence. Was it a mouse? Or a raccoon? It sounded larger, like a dog. One morning, as Mrs.

Haunted Estill County

Walters was walking to the restroom, the rather large dog met her on the stairs. Startled, she took a second look; they didn't own a dog! But he had disappeared.

As time went by the Walters found out they were expecting. Hauntings can have a way of altering when there is change in the house and this one was of no exception. One afternoon while Susan, months along in her pregnancy, was walking down the stairs an invisible hand pushed her from behind, nearly sending her sprawling on her stomach. When she was pregnant with her second child, it happened again. For the rest of her pregnancy she avoided the stairs, fearful of what might happen if she didn't catch herself.

There wasn't any logical explanation for these happenings in the Walters' house. There had been no previous ghost stories about the place and while they weren't disbelievers in the paranormal, they were also surprised at the intensity of what was occurring.

Then, one night, Susan began dreaming about

the woman. With her long dark hair and burned skin, she stood in a room shaped like a steeple. Mirrors surrounded her. The dream haunted Susan in more ways than one. Not only did she find it incredibly disturbing, but it filled her with questions. Who was the woman? What did she want? Where was the room located and what did it mean?

Renovations were needed on the home and after a time of pulling up boards and tearing into walls, a journal was discovered. It was more than eighty years old and Susan was startled to find an image of the writer–a woman with long dark hair that bore a striking resemblance to the one in her dreams. The journal itself revealed another secret; an upstairs bedroom had been full of mirrors at one time. The mysterious writer had also kept a menagerie of animals she had loved to death, quite literally as it turned out. Fascinated, Susan continued to read. The couple had been unable to have any children and when the writer proved to be barren her husband had left her.

The house, located more than six miles from the nearest neighbor, was lonely and isolating for the woman who was left there to live alone.

Intrigued, Susan spent the next several weeks conducting her own research. The house had been set on fire and the top floor nearly destroyed. Bits of broken mirrors looked not as if they had exploded in the fire but had been smashed with a heavy, blunt object. She had died in the fire, but her husband had returned, restored the former upstairs, and sold it.

Having solved the mystery of the woman and the house Susan felt a sense of relief, at least temporarily. The noises stopped and the singing was never heard again. Some afternoons, though, when the light was just right, a woman with long dark hair in a white lace dress could be seen standing in one of the upstairs windows.

Irvine: A Hotbed for UFO Activity?

Although we've become accustomed to seeing accounts of UFOs and extraterrestrials as they pay visits to rural dwellers, these adventures are normally plastered all over the tabloids and paranormal websites and generally take place in isolated desert regions that are far-removed from the mountains and shadowy valleys of Estill County.

It might come as a surprise, then, to some that Irvine and Ravenna have both seen their own fair share of UFO activity, although it might not be a surprise to those who live there.

Haunted Estill County

On a cool September night, Joe and Elizabeth were out on their front porch near Stacy Lane. It had been a long day at work for both of them and they were glad to be home, resting. Suddenly, a flash of light appeared off in the distance. "What was that?" Elizabeth asked.

Looked like somebody taking a picture," Joe shrugged. A few seconds later, it happened again–this time a multiple of flashes in rapid succession.

"Must be taking a lot of pictures, huh?" Elizabeth remarked.

"Too low to the ground to be an airplane or anything," Joe said, although it wasn't uncommon to see helicopters or small engines fly over the area, headed toward the Bluegrass Army Depot at this time of night.

All at once, the flash appeared again, this time much closer. Instead of diminishing, however, it appeared to grow larger, as though it was traveling

Haunted Estill County

closer to their porch. The light wasn't the red color most noticeable on aircraft carriers or the bright yellow of a camera flash; rather it was greenish with just the hint of blue surrounding it.

"What the hell?" Elizabeth screamed, throwing her Coke can on the floor and darting into the house, slamming the screen door behind her.

Joe, more curious than afraid, stayed and watched. In amazement, the light seemed to be able to see him. Feeling as though he was being watched, he walked down his steps and out into his yard. He figured the light was about three miles away and possibly two-hundred feet up in the air. It wasn't a large presence, but it was bright. Surely everyone else outside could see it as well?

Several minutes went by and he continued to watch it, contemplating its meaning. Then, as quickly as it had appeared, it was gone. It didn't move to another location as much as it simply dissipated into the air and was no longer visible.

Stacy Lane is no stranger to unusual events. In fact, a black moving blog had been recently sighted at the Crows Curve and it was known for being host to several unexplainable automobile accidents.

***

One week later, on Sandhill, another couple would be in their front yard, bringing the groceries in from the car, when they also saw a bright light in the sky. In the five minutes it took them to walk back and forth to their house and unload their bags, the bright, vibrant light never moved.

"It's a star or a planet, right?" Jennifer asked her boyfriend. "Like the North Star or Saturn or something?"

"Maybe…" he replied, uncertainly. Secretly, he was pretty sure it wasn't the North Star and as for being a planet it looked awfully close to the ground. As he gazed at the light and the stars around him, it occurred to him, as it had on many recent occasions the sky looked different these days. The Big Dipper wasn't the same shape he remembered it being as a child, but then he imagined all things appear to children differently than they do to adults. He'd lived in Richmond for the past fifteen years and chalked the difference up to finally being back in the country again, where the lights from the city didn't darken up the night sky as much.

Suddenly, the light began to move. As they watched in wonder, it turned from a bright yellow color to a distinctively reddish hue. Slowly, it started its movement toward the west. "It's a plane," they said in unison and then laughed. Their laughter faded when its speed picked up and the light grew three times in size and began racing through the night sky, its pace so fast it became nothing but a blur leaving a red streak in its wake.

***

Most everyone is accustomed to the description of bright, moving lights and low aircrafts that are just a little too fast and a little too oddly shaped to be regular planes, but sometimes the object is so peculiar there's not even a good way to describe it at all.

It was still chilly in the late May evening when Justice and her friends sat out on her front step, drinking Ale-8s and smoking. She and her mother had been fighting for months over her cigarettes, but it was a losing battle. Finally, they had reached an agreement of sorts: Justice had to pay for them herself and could only smoke outside.

The school week had been long but the year was almost over and she and her friends were looking forward to a long summer ahead of them. At the age of fifteen, she wasn't really old enough yet to have a real job and part of her knew this might be the last real summer of her childhood. She intended to see it go out with a bang.

Laughing and giggling, the girls talked about the trips to Richmond they would take, the movies they would rent, which house they might be able to score beer at, and which guy was either single or would be by the time their real summer started.

It's hard to say who first became aware of the black shape in the distance, but when the conversation finally slid off to the side and the air became quiet they all realized they were staring at it.

From where they were sitting, it might have been a large black cloud. The full moon lit up both Justice's yard and the sky and sometimes the low-lying clouds took on menacing appearances, especially when teenage girls, giggles, and late night talks were combined. This was no cloud, though. The shape was too dark, too circular, and too out of place to be anything natural.

Haunted Estill County

Slowly, the mass began inching its way across the sky, picking up momentum as it seemed to circle over some rooftops and linger momentarily before racing off to the next.

"It's like it's looking for something," one of the girls whispered.

As though it had heard her, the mass stopped moving and bobbed. "Oh my God," Justice squealed. "What the hell *is* that anyway?"

All of the girls quickly rose to their feet, but none could muster up the motivation to go inside. They were too curious and still maintained a tiny slice of common sense that told them they really must be looking at some natural phenomenon they had just never seen before.

For nearly five minutes they watched as the mass circled Justice's roof, swayed in the airless night, and expanded upon itself, only to slide back into the circular shape. At last, it appeared to lose interest in the girls and the house and moved on, fading into the night sky.

***

Irvine's UFO phenomenon has not gone unnoticed by the national media. In 1978, the *National Enquirer* ran an article about the UFO activity in central Kentucky and mentioned Irvine several times.

According to the article, a 16-year-old by the name of Terry Kirby from Irvine was apparently chopping wood when a glowing oval-shaped UFO came into view. Not only was the UFO highly visible from Kirby's location, a picture was even taken of the event. He stated the object was "as big as a house."

Marcus Cole, the police chief at the time, was quoted as saying there were several eyewitnesses who had seen "flying saucers in Irvine." The publisher of *The Citizen Voice & Times*, Guy Hatfield, stated in the article that those who had seen the spectacles were all

Haunted Estill County

"solid citizens, with no reason to say it unless they saw one."

The article went on to say that Kentucky State Trooper, Jim Whitaker saw a UFO with red/white/blue/green pulsating lights the size of a car hovering over a field in Irvine. According to Mr. Whitaker, it definitely was not an airplane or a helicopter. For two hours, the state trooper chased the object through the dark. According to Whitaker, when an aircraft approached it, "the intensity of its lights would die down... and once the aircraft was clear, it would light up again!"

***

Yet another police officer is recorded as seeing a UFO in Irvine as well, this time in 1988. According to a Mufon report, on August 25th, the officer was watching traffic when a large Delta-shaped object came into view. It came from the southwest and was heading northeast. There were collision lights on all three corners and was at least two-hundred feet in the air. The observer, who had been an officer for thirty years, stated he had "no nonsense in [his] life and work." He was about one hundred yards from his home at the time and his wife, who was taking a bath at the time, had her water disturbed by ripples.

The officer claimed other members of the community saw the UFO at the same time. One man, who lived on a nearby mountain, claimed the object was "searching" the hills.

***

So what are the lights being seen all over Estill County? Are they signs of extraterrestrial life on other planets? Are they demons or spirits that have wandered over from another dimension or a parallel universe, intent on gathering information and generally wreck havoc on those who don't follow their wishes?

Some are sure the frequency of these unidentified objects is a sign the End Times are coming. Many believe that rather than being aliens from another galaxy, these are demonic beings that are evil in nature and bring messages of death and destruction. There are those who remember Christ said other messiahs would come in His name and they're concerned these creatures will try to deceive those around them into believing they are, in fact, Him.

There are others, though, who believe perhaps these creatures are not coming for malevolent purposes but are, instead, showing others the gateways to Heaven, Hell, and Purgatory. After all, if angels and demons live amongst us then shouldn't they have a means of traveling as well?

Haunted Estill County

The Music Never Stopped

Several years ago, my family moved to Estill County and rented a house near Thomas Road. The house itself wasn't an old one, but like many places in the county, the area around it was old and rife with history.

A common misconception regarding Kentucky history is that Indians never lived here in permanent settlements. Now we know this isn't true. There

Haunted Estill County

were many camps and a couple of permanent settlements scattered throughout the modern day state. The Shawnee, in particular, favored Estill County.

We had been living in our new house for several months when I first started getting a spooky vibe. As a writer, I often work late at night and sometimes all the way through the night if I need to. I prefer the stillness and the quietness, although on a couple of occasions I have managed to spook myself and ended the night earlier than anticipated because I couldn't stand to sit up alone any longer.

One morning, at around 3:00 am, I became aware of a very gentle voice singing nearby. The sound was so distinct and clear I didn't question it. Indeed, after a couple of minutes of listening to it I could very nearly hum along with the tune. The words were indistinguishable but didn't sound English. The voice, low and smooth, was a man's. I continued to listen to the singing for about another hour as I finished my work and wrapped things up for the night.

I had completely forgotten about the music until my mother brought it up later the next day. Was I playing something on the computer last night? She, too, had heard the singing. To her, it sounded as though it was coming from upstairs where my office was located.

Two nights later, I was up late again and halfway through the night, the music started back. This time, there were more voices joined together to create what I could only consider to be a chanting of sorts. It wasn't melodic, but it had a certain rhythm to it that made it catchy. I listened to it for a few minutes and then went downstairs and pecked on my mother's bedroom door. "Do you hear that?" I asked. She sat up and listened. She did.

Although the music was slightly fainter downstairs, it could still be heard. "Maybe it's coming from somewhere down in the valley and we're just picking it up," I suggested.

Haunted Estill County

So, wrapping a blanket around me, I opened the front door and stepped out onto the porch. The music had stopped. No sounds emerged from the nighttime other than crickets and frogs. As soon as I stepped back inside the house, though, it began again.

"It still sounds like it's coming from upstairs," my mother said. She was right, it did.

Outside doors to my office lead to a small balcony. I stood there and listened. Surely, if the music was echoing off the mountains, I would be able to hear it. I couldn't. Shutting the doors, I went back inside and sat back down at the computer.

Moments later, the music began again. This time it was slow, sad. The lyrics were still indistinguishable but the melody was lonesome. Another trip around the upstairs showed me no radios, televisions, or CD players had been left on. My son's musical toys were all quiet. Whatever the music was, it was only coming to my office and didn't seem to have a presence much anywhere else.

For the longest time, I sat there and listened to it. The mournful sound was hollow and low. It triggered something in me that made me sad but I couldn't put my finger on what it was.

A few nights later, it came back.

Past the point of being afraid, I decided to do some research on the area. Calling on my husband, who had once worked with Native American history of the local area, we did our own investigating.

Station Camp, one of Daniel Boone's first settlements, was located somewhere nearby. Although a sign points to it from the McDonald's in town, nobody really knows where it was. Could it have been closer to our house than I thought? And, if so, were we picking up on some remnants of an old Longhunter's camp?

There were Native American settlements in the area. One of the largest permanent ones was located in what is now Kiddville. There was fighting in this area, too. Could I have been picking up on some lost souls wandering around the hills in the woods and trying to find their way back?

For nearly a year I listened to the music in my office. Sometimes it was louder than others; the chanting and staccato notes filling the room with a rhythm that made me want to type faster and swing my legs. Other times it was slow, gentle, and sad. A few times I found myself closing my eyes, tears streaming down my cheeks for a memory I didn't even seem to have.

That next summer I had a son. A cradle was placed in my office so he could nap while I worked. One morning, after I showered, I went into the room to wake him up and get him dressed. He was cold and blue, having passed away in his sleep.

The music never played again.

On the Line

Of course, not all haunted houses are to be discovered in the countryside. Some of the most intriguing places are right in the center of town.

For outsiders, there might not be a clear distinction between where one of our towns ends and the other begins but for the locals those lines are more than just signs. One of the spookiest haunted houses is right on a line separating the two towns and has provided fodder for ghost stories for years.

Many people have ties to this large, old home and more than one person has shared their ghost story about it over the years. During the day, you can hear furniture moving throughout the rooms, doors opening and closing by uninvited guests, and the echoes of children's giggles floating down the hallway.

At night, the presence has taken on a more sinister energy that has not been limited to the awareness of adults. Children have claimed to see shadowy figures come into their bedroom, only to move items and watch them as they pretended to sleep. A malevolent presence that beckons from a dark, drafty closet has caught more than one child off guard.

For many years, the home's occupant was a fortune teller. Reading her tea leaves and coffee grounds, she provided answers to those who came to her, seeking news of their past and future. Some believe practicing these arts can open a door between the realms and allow spirits to pass through, unobstructed. Others who were in the house before this occupant claim to have heard things even before her searching into the lives of others was forayed.

What has caused these hauntings? For some

years the house was a nursing home. The bell of an elderly woman who would use it to gain the attention of an attendant continued to ring long after her death. Stories of a woman committing suicide in an upstairs room swirl around the house and are attributed to the haunting. And what unseen, yet malevolent, force is felt from inside one of the closets? These answers might never be known.

Standing on the line between these two towns, you might feel as though you are being pulled in two different directions at once. Perhaps that's how these spirits feel–unable to determine which world they would rather be in.

Haunted Estill County

Abandoned house near Sandhill

The Ghost of the Headless Timberman

For years, timber was the number one industry in Estill County. Many people moved to the area to work in the hills. Although the woods eventually couldn't hold up to the demand and the county never really say the fruits of its labor, for awhile it did provide some jobs.

During the late 1800s, there was a boom in this industry and a sawmill was built on Sandhill Road. Dozens found jobs there and, in the evenings and on breaks, had to find ways to find amusement. Card playing, practical jokes, and storytelling were all ways to pass the time and get to know one another.

Haunted Estill County

One night, however, a particular card game got out of hand. As moonshine was consumed and tempers flared, in anger, one of men began waving his knife around. Unfortunately, the knife found the head of an innocent bystander. Being recently sharpened, it made contact with the man's neck and beheaded him on the spot. He was able to run out of the room and collapsed on the ground as the others watched in horror.

The Headless Timberman has been spotted in those parts by many people over the years. For some, he steps out onto the road before them, confused and disoriented, arms flailing as blood gushes from his neck. For others, the apparition is more menacing as he claws at them and grabs in a desperate attempt to be saved from his awful fate.

The Case of the Mysterious Government Agent

Estill County might see its share of state troopers and other law enforcement as they pass through the county, usually heading toward the Mountain Parkway, but it doesn't exactly get its fair share of CIA, FBI, or other types of government agents. What, then, was the Secret Service agent doing on top of the mountain outside of Irvine and how did he really die? And, does his spirit still haunt the hills that must have been foreign to him?

Haunted Estill County

Gary Joe Bergsen was a Secret Service officer, originally from Spotsylvania County in Virginia. In September 1990, he was found dead in the Mountain Springs Cemetery in the Daniel Boone National Forest. The cause of death was a gunshot wound and it was eventually ruled a suicide. Why was he in the isolated cemetery to begin with, though, and what connection did he have to Estill County?

Located in Furnace, the cemetery itself is close to the Estill County-Powell County line. It's a small cemetery and no link has ever been established between it and the mysterious government agent. Mark Rupert, who was the Secret Service spokesman at the time, told the *Washington Post* Gary was on annual leave at the time of his death and was not in Kentucky on any kind of official business. No one had any idea as to why he might be in Kentucky at all, much less in the Appalachian Mountains in a rural cemetery. Before his death, he had been in California, apparently visiting

Haunted Estill County

family there. He had gone on a hunting trip and his equipment was still left in the vehicle he was found dead in. His sister, who had seen him shortly before his death, said he was happy and excited about work when she had last spoken to him.

The agent, who had been driving a pick-up truck, was found sitting behind the wheel. Kentucky State Trooper Ed Robinson told the Fredericksburg *Free-Lance Star* evidence pointed towards Agent Bergsen committing suicide with his .38 pistol. The bullet that killed him was from the gun in his hand. His fingerprints were the only one found on the gun. This appeared straightforward, if you manage to ignore the fact that his reasons for being in the cemetery were unclear, but the state trooper was worried about one little detail: the sightings of a 1976 Ford Sedan with Virginia license plates seen in the area earlier that day. As most people can attest, it's rare to see an out of state car in the Estill County back roads, especially one nobody knows.

In a weird twist of fate, on the same day Gary's body was found in his pickup truck in Irvine, his stolen Jeep was found in Lexington. It was parked in front of a church and still had the keys in the ignition. Gary had reported it missing in 1987.

The story does get a little bit stranger from here on out. In 1992, two years after his death, his old neighbors complained about his empty house and the derelict state it was in. The house, located in Fredericksburg, Virginia, was empty but had been purchased by Carl Schleicher and Alton Perkins not long after the agent's death. Both of these men belonged to an organization called the Mankind Research Foundation. According to Schleicher, the organization's intent was to offer low-cost housing options. However, additional research shows the organization is involved in research, psychology experiments, and biocommunications.

Haunted Estill County

It's possible, of course, the newspaper was incorrect in reporting the organization's mission. It's also possible it was entirely a coincidence the people who bought the house had anything to do with parapsychological happenings and the agent's death or life in general. It is probably just as much of a coincidence that some of the members of the Willoughby family are buried in that cemetery; Loretta Willoughby, of course, being the young girl murdered in Irvine whose case has never been solved.

Initially, investigators thought he might have come upon some illegal marijuana plants or farmers and had been killed. With the self-inflicted gunshot wound, however, this does not seem likely. His family in California figured he had gone through Kentucky on his way back to Virginia and had camped out along the way.

The specifics around this case are not really known. Research brings up conflicting information.

Haunted Estill County

Was he shot in the neck? In the back of the head? Was the old church nearby that has since burned down used for satanic rituals? Was he meeting someone there as part of a secret government operation? Or, was he simply stressed from the pressures of his job and wanted an out? These questions might never been answered. Still, stories have circulated for many years now that a single gunshot can be heard in the early morning hours if the weather is just right near the narrow lane that runs by the cemetery.

South Irvine Tragedy

Many of the most horrific and saddest ghost stories involve hauntings by children. We normally associate ghosts with those individuals who had unfinished business or ties to a place they don't want to let go of. With children, however, we like to think of them as having moved on; alighting to a place where there is joy and happiness and comfort. There is something both frightening and sad about the idea of a child holding onto an earthly dwelling, stuck in a purgatory of sorts, where time is standing still for them.

Most of the hauntings involving children are but faint echoes. Perhaps they aren't really ghosts at all, but

Haunted Estill County

leftover energy clinging to the walls and floors of the children who once inhabited the place. Not all ghosts are spirits that are able to interact with the living; some are holograms of a sort merely reflecting something once alive. Is it better to think of ghost children in this manner? Are their footsteps and cries just vestiges of past sounds and nothing more than whispers on our earthly plane? Or, are they really unable to pass over and their cries sounds for help that cannot be answered?

There is a house in South Irvine that is inhabited by the spirit of a young boy. In many of the ghost stories involving children, illness and sudden death are no strangers to the life of a child. A prolonged illness in a child might produce fear and suffering and it's possible these things remain even after the child is gone. Or, it could be the child passed away so quickly they don't yet know they are dead.

In mountain cultures like our own, it's common

to call on the grace of God to heal those who are suffering from sickness. Modern medicines have their place but many believe God's will is stronger and prayer is more healing than anything that can be found in a doctor's office or hospital.

In the South Irvine tragedy, a young boy was suffering from pneumonia. As his illness progressed and the boy became sicker and sicker, it became obvious the home remedies were not helping him–he needed the help of a doctor. His father, however, was a religious man and believed the power of God would save his son and have mercy on his family.

The young boy was not healed by the power of God, however, and died in his own home. Today, the old house is home to more than just its living inhabitants. At night, when the sun has gone down and everyone is tucked safely inside for the evening, the sound of little footsteps running back and forth across the wooden floorboards can be heard. Is the young boy

Haunted Estill County

still playing in his childhood home? Or is the house itself just remembering a happier time?

An Accidental Murder

It's not always easy to get along with the in-laws, but sometimes what starts out as a simple disagreement can fester over time and build until it becomes out of control. In rare cases, arguments that started out small can even end in death. This is what happened on Crooked Creek in the 19th century.

Tucked away in the hills around Crooked Creek was a house that was home to a man and his daughter. The mother had long since passed on when the daughter married. Together, the newlyweds continued to live with the young woman's father.

As can happen, the father and new husband

didn't see eye to eye on many things and, after awhile, their arguments began escalating. The addition to the new family, a son, did little to ease the friction that was mounting in the house.

By some accounts, the husband himself was not the best of spouses, although whether he was unfaithful to his young wife or simply a scoundrel of the time is unclear. In any event, he decided to pack up and leave her and their son and head out west.

Before he could pack his bags and leave Irvine, however, the young woman's father heard tale of his plans and decided to thwart his attempt at abandonment. After all, he might not like the fellow but he was married to his daughter and he had sworn to protect and support her when they married.

The confrontation itself took place outside the house. The daughter and her son were tucked safely inside but could see the argument escalating from the front window. As the father and son-in-law fought with one another, things went from bad to worse. Finally, in rage, the older man pulled out his gun and tried to shoot his daughter's husband. Unfortunately, he missed and the bullet intended for the other man went past him and through the window where his daughter was standing. The stray bullet hit the baby she was holding, passed through him, and went into her own heart. Both died immediately, leaving the two men alone with one another.

For many years after their deaths, at night passing visitors could still see the outline of a young woman, holding a baby, standing in the window of the house. When the house burned down years later, the ghostly vision of the little family disappeared with it, but the sounds of the baby's cries can still often be heard soaring through the night.

The Ghostly Passenger

Many towns across the country have their tales of special roads that ghostly hitchhikers travel down, waiting for the car that will pick them up and carry them on to their intended destinations. Estill County is no different in this aspect; here, too, is a ghostly passenger searching for her ride.

Highway 52 runs throughout Estill County, connecting it to both Madison County in the west and Lee County in the east. The western part of the road is wide with multiple lanes in some areas. It is well maintained and a busy stretch of road. On the eastern

Haunted Estill County

side, however, one could travel several miles through the winding stretch up the mountain and never encounter a single vehicle. The road gets narrower in places as the mountains seemingly close in on it and the real beauty of Estill County unfolds as the trees open up to reveal an almost ethereal valley below.

It is on this part of the road the ghostly passenger awaits her drivers.

As the road winds up onto the mountaintop and snakes through the trees, the elevation climbs higher and higher. You could almost imagine that you slipped through time as there are few houses and almost no signs of development. Some travelers claim to have felt a pull along this stretch of pavement and, when they reached the bottom, wondered where they had really just been. It can feel like another world up there.

At the top of the mountain, it's possible that another world does briefly open for those who dare to welcome it. Stopping your vehicle and opening your door might just allow you to pick up a passenger that you'll feel but never see. In the steep curve of this road, a woman waits, lonely for the man or woman who will help her travel down the side of the mountain. If you choose to transport her down the mountainside, however, you must be sure to stop your car and let her out when you reach the bottom. If you fail to do this, you might find that you have a crash yourself on down the road.

The woman's story is not known. The rumors are that she crashed in the curve years and years ago and continues to haunt the area that she died in, unable to find her way back home. The road can be a dangerous one and, close to the quarry, there is a crashed vehicle which stands to the testament of the dangers of this particular spot. But does she really travel back and forth every night and wait for someone who will save her and help her reach her home?

Myth or Truth?

Sometimes it's hard to tell where the real story ends and the urban legend begins. Over the years, a story can get twisted and turned so much that it barely resembles the original truth. The more a haunted house story gets told, the more the story changes. Sometimes, even the original story behind the haunting can change. Sometimes the person was murdered, other times they committed suicide. In one version it might be a child haunting the house and in another an old woman.

In some cases, the tale gets so twisted the exact location of the supposed haunting can't even be pinpointed. You'll be just as sure it's the red house at the end of the road as someone else is sure it's the white one at the beginning. So goes the Sandhill haunting story.

There is a farm on Sandhill. The exact location of this farm is not known, since it has a tendency to change depending on the person who is telling the story. The one thing that everyone can agree on is that the house is old, rests on a farm, and that something terrible happened there and that energy still clings to the property.

Those who claim to have visited the farm (or think they have the right place, anyhow) all say the same thing: the powerful surge of evil is overwhelming. Some have walked away with an uneasy feeling they find they can't brush off until they're safely back on HWY 52. Others feel an overpowering sense of dread that has them calling their loved ones to check on them, sure that something must be wrong. Still, others have walked away feeling such a perverse sense of evil emanating from the house that they are never really able to travel back to that area again.

Some have driven past the property and felt so uneasy they find themselves hitting the gas in order to get back to HWY 52. Others have noticed shadow people out of the corners of their eyes. More than one person has had their car stall for no discernible reason in front of the property.

So what happened at this house and why is the energy that leaks from it so negative? Some say that it has to do with foster children being murdered. Others say that a horrible man lived there years and years ago and murdered his wife and daughter. Still others claim that it was the owner's son who went on a rampage, killing several people in the community.

Although the story changes considerably, it always ends the same way: the bodies are buried at the bottom of the pond and "trophies" of the victims are scattered around the farm.

Is this Irvine's very own serial killer? Are severed hands, legs, feet, and even heads buried haphazardly under the fields and in the house's cellar? Who was this man and why did he cut the bodies up to begin with? Some say that he was fascinated with the mob and wanted to be a hitman when he was younger. Severing the hands of a victim was something that gangsters were said to have done long ago, mostly to help keep the victims from being identified.

The Shadow People

Sometimes old phenomenon starts being known under a new name. That might be the case with what is now being called the "shadow people" and Estill County has become a hotbed of activity for them. These beings are not just limited to old, spooky houses and cemeteries. In fact, many of the sightings have been around restaurants, storefronts, and newer developments that didn't even have prior residents.

During the course of collecting these stories I

was presented with many different tales of shadow people in Estill County. Some were exhaustive encounters that lasted off and on for years. Others were shorter descriptions of shadowy figures the storyteller merely caught out of the corner of their eye, but left them feeling nervous and uneasy. Here, I am including a few of those stories.

For many years Jenny Maynard thought that she might be going crazy. As a young child she became distinctly aware of a shadowy presence that seemed to follow her everywhere she went. For a long time, she brushed this figure off as simply being what it looked like–her shadow. Yet, over time, she realized that it couldn't possibly be connected to the sun's rays. For one thing, it appeared even when there wasn't enough light to cast a shadow.

Soon, she began talking to it. After all, her

grandmother had always told her that if you saw a ghost you should speak to it and ask it what it wanted. So she tried speaking to it, asking it what it wanted, and generally being friendly toward the apparition. It never answered back, or even changed, but those around her began making fun of this strange communication.

    Fear eventually canceled out curiosity and Jenny stopped talking to the shadowy figure that seemed to follow her, hide around every corner, and even lurk near people in crowds. She tried to ignore it, thinking that it could be her attention that was keeping it nearby, but the figure didn't ease away. Sometimes she became so frightened that she would shut herself in a dark room. The presence didn't seem to like the dark, ironically enough, and that was the only relief she got from it.

    As an adult the encounters became less frequent and suddenly one year she noticed that she hadn't seen the figure in quite some time.

Ricky Marcum would not consider himself a superstitious man and, when asked, he would still tell you that he's not sure there are such things as "ghosts." He is quite sure, however, that he has seen the shadow people around Estill County.

He first became aware of them as an adult although when he thinks back on his childhood he admits that he might have seen them before, but only as quick traces out of the corner of his eye. Like Jenny, he describes them in much the same way: tall, dark, and with the shape of a human.

The first time Ricky really got a good look at the figures was actually downtown on Main Street. He was coming out of a store and felt the needle pricks on his arm that raced up to his hairline; someone was watching him. When he turned around, a large black mass stood about twenty feet from him. It was the shape of a tall human, possibly a man, but as he watched it, it slowly melted into the wall next to where it had stood. He was chilled, but figured that it must have been a shadow caused by the setting sun.

A few months later he would see it again. This time he was working outside and, again, the chills ran up his arm and into his hairline where it felt like every hair on his scalp stood at attention. When he turned around, the shadowy figure was close to his front door, lingering, and watching him. As he started walking toward it, it disappeared.

This is not something he felt comfortable sharing with anyone. He didn't want them to think he was crazy. Over the course of the next several years, however, the shadowy figure made multiple appearances. There was never anything nearby that could have caused the shadow to form naturally and each time he saw it he felt as though it was watching him, and waiting.

Haunted Estill County

Lucy Evans has no doubt the shadow people exist. In fact, she has seen them all her life. She can't remember a time when she didn't see them: on the stairs of her house, leaning against storefronts as she walked by, and even slithering around popular restaurants like the Wig Wam and the Twin. Although they often appear to her in crowds, nobody else ever seems aware of them. She is convinced they are not tied to the places she sees them, but that they follow her.

For a long time she didn't know what to call them. For awhile she referred to them as "shape shifters" since, upon closer inspection, they would often slip and slide and become taller, wider, or even take on the form of an animal. Her grandmother told her they were demons and that she should stay away from them. Her preacher told her, as a child, there were no such things as demons so she wondered if they weren't angels for a time.

Haunted Estill County

She does not feel relaxed around them and finds them menacing.

There have been times in her life when the sightings of these shadow people have been so numerous that she is afraid to venture outside on sunny days. Like Jenny, she noticed they seem to be afraid of dark places. A few years ago she treated her house with burnt sage and laid brick dust and salt in front of all her
entrances. She hasn't seen the figures inside her home since.

That doesn't mean that she doesn't still see them in public, however. In crowds she can sometimes see them standing close to other people, watching and listening. For awhile she wondered if perhaps she was crazy. She even talked to a neurologist who checked her for seizures. Nothing was discovered. Eventually, though, she began searching for what she was seeing on a regular occurrence online and was startled to find websites centered around these strange beings. For the first time since she was a little girl, she felt less alone.

Julia Means lived grew up in Richmond but her grandparents still lived on a farm on Red Lick when she was growing up. Throughout her childhood, she would spend the night with them and loved sleeping in the big featherbed and waking up in the morning to feed the goats and collect the eggs from the chickens. At around the age of eight, however, she became aware of the shadowy figures that lurked around the farm and for the first time ever she grew scared of the rambling farmhouse and expanse of acreage.

The first time it happened, she was in bed and almost asleep. Her grandmother had left a lamp on for her and the soft light cast shadows across the walls. She found this comforting, as she was afraid of the dark. One night, however, as she was drifting off, she noticed that one of the shadows on the wall began growing. It started off very small and the longer she watched it, the taller it grew. Curious, she looked around the bedroom to see what might be causing the shadow. There wasn't anything that was likely. A little afraid, she covered her head up with her blanket and fell asleep.

The next night, she was in bed when she became aware of something entering the room. Expecting to see her grandmother, she opened her eyes and smiled. Instead, it was a shadowy figure that first walked toward the fireplace and then silently crept toward her bed. Frightened, she jumped out of bed and ran down the hall.

From then on, Julia always slept with the light off. Even as an adult she needs to have blackout curtains and complete darkness to be able to sleep.

In 2002, a young woman was in her basement, doing her laundry. Her basement was a place that many of her friends had found creepy in the past, but it had never bothered her, despite her overactive imagination. On this night, she was alone and the sun had just sunk behind the mountains.

With her back to the staircase, she folded laundry and put in a new load. Suddenly, she became aware of something watching her. She was so certain that when she turned around she would see one of her roommates standing at the foot of the stairs that she was surprised when she turned and found nobody.

Moments later, it happened again.

This time, when she turned around, she was startled to see a tall figure standing just a few yards from her. The figure had no distinct features. It had the shape of a person with its extremities that could have been arms and a round point at its top which she took for its head. It appeared to be wearing a cloak, however, and this drug to the ground. It was shrouded completely in black.

In frozen fear, she watched the figure as it

seemed to watch her. After a couple of seconds, the shadowy figure moved away from the stairs and went on into the deeper part of the basement. The walk is something that she will never forget, however. The figure did not seem to glide or move with feet, but made a bobbing motion that was slow and deliberate. For some reason, its movements frightened her more than the sight of the figure itself.

She knew without a doubt that the figure had seen her. It had been aware of her as much as she had been aware of it. She never saw it again.

So who are the shadow people? Or, perhaps more aptly, *what* are they? Some people think their appearance in Estill County has become more pronounced in the past few years. More and more people are increasingly talking about spotting them—even those who do not claim to believe in the supernatural.

There are different theories regarding their origins.

Some believe they might be fallen angels. Others think they might be demons. In most cases, the witness has felt afraid and felt a malevolent force surrounding them. Indeed, many observers have been able to vanquish these beings by praying aloud. The nephilum were fallen angels and giants of their time. After being cast out of Heaven, they proceeded to breed with the human race. In most of the reported cases of the shadow people, they appear to women who are still of childbearing age.

Sometimes, the beings appear aggressive towards those who see them. There are reports of attacks and even attempted suffocation, lending those in paranormal research to believe the shadow people are not merely observers but are here for a specific purpose. With that in mind, there are those who think they might be aliens sent here to watch us and learn from us.

Of course, they often get categorized with ghosts, although most who have seen them say they are far different than other ghostly figures they have seen. In most of the reported ghost sightings, the observer has been able to see clothing, human details in the face, and can distinguish the gender. In the shadow people, none of this is discernible.

Lastly, there are those who think they might be inter-dimensional beings or even astral bodies. If there are parallel universes to our own, then is it possible that, from time to time, those hazy lines can become even more confused and beings can slip over into the other realm? If that's the case, then perhaps we appear as shadow people to others.

The Haunting of Barnes Mountain

As one of the highest and most isolated peaks in the county, Barnes Mountain looms over the valleys and fields of southern Estill County. Over the years there have been scores of stories surrounding the mountain and its inhabitants, not all of them ghost stories, but its oftentimes murky reputation isn't recent. Barnes Mountain has an interesting past that goes back nearly to the inception of Estill County and its original inhabitants.

Cemeteries, with their crumbling tombstones and permeable silence, are some of the scariest places to visit after dark. It's not just the atmosphere that spooks some folks, however. Many people have taken seemingly normal pictures in Estill County cemeteries, only to go home and look at them later, surprised at the multitude of orbs, shadows, and even ghostly figures that emerge in their images. Sometimes, the camera picks up things that are nearly imperceptible to the human eye.

There is one such cemetery on Barnes Mountain that has been host to several different ghostly experiences to visitors over the years. One woman, for instance, took a seemingly innocent picture of a relative's headstone, only to have the film developed later to see the image of a shadowy figure of a woman holding an infant near the grave.

There is also a grave of a young boy that has gotten a lot of interest, both from paranormal researchers and "regular" visitors alike. The grave is an old one, and slightly crumbling, but if you stand next to it with a tape recorder and talk to it you might be surprised at what you hear when you play it back. More than one person has heard voices other than their own. Others have taken pictures of the grave, only to return home and find eerie images of small hands, feet, and even eyes peering back at them.

Those who have ventured into the graveyard after midnight have even purportedly seen drops of blood oozing from some of the headstones. Although some people believe the spirits of those who have passed on don't haunt their earthly burial places, others believe those who passed on too soon or in a violent manner might still be tied to the places where their bodies rest. There is evidence of Native American camps in the surrounding Estill County hills and many think that some of the most haunted locations on Barnes Mountain are in close proximity to burial grounds of our ancient ancestors.

Haunted Estill County

Haunted graveyards are not the only ghostly places on Barnes Mountain, of course. There are at least two caves that reportedly see ghostly activity as well. One of them has to do with a well-known murder and subsequent trial. The other is lesser known, and may be chalked up to urban legend, but it's nevertheless a sad and haunting tale.

In 1905, on Doe Creek, George Lunsford was intoxicated as he made his way home. His father was upset upon George's arrival and made a point in calling him out for his drunken behavior. In agitation, he reproached George by saying, "George, I am too old a man to have you coming home drunk, and I can't put up with it." Whether in drunkenness or mere anger, George pulled out his revolver and shot at his father. Luckily, the bullet just grazed his head and landed in a clock on the fireplace mantle. However, his father'd had two visitors that evening: William and Irvine Manus (sometimes spelled Manness). Upon George's shooting, one of the brothers cried, "Why George, I wouldn't do that." This seemed to upset George even more for he then began shooting at the brothers themselves.

Both received serious wounds with the death shots being to their stomachs. One developed peritonitis and the other remained in critical condition upon the arrival of the doctors who came that Sunday night. Because the brothers were so highly respected in the community, it didn't take long for people to start talking about lynching George.

George, almost immediately realizing the gravity of his actions, quickly ran from the house and hid. He was finally caught by the sheriff who found him hiding in a cave on Barnes Mountain. *The Mount Vernon Signal* reported that he was "not taken until after a hard fight." He was subsequently put in the Irvine jail where he waited for his trial. In the meantime, the sheriff made sure the jail had a lot of protection, fearing that harm would come to George before he could be legally tried. This was probably a good thing because it wasn't long before someone called from Rice Station, alerting the sheriff that a crowd of at least fifty people were heading toward Irvine–angry and looking for George. *The Richmond Climax* reported that Dick Johnson, the jailer, was "a determined and fearless man" and that he declared he would not "give up [his] prisoner to any mob."

News of the murder even made *The New York Sun* in October of 1905. The paper's caption, "Want to Lynch Murderer", talked about the murder and the angry mob that was now surrounding the jail, possibly numbering in the hundreds. However, while the paper called the murder "cold blooded", it also made the mistake of saying that it was his brother that he initially shot at, and not his father.

On December 29, 1905, *The Interior Journal* out of Stanford reported that George Lunsford had received a life sentence by the Irvine circuit court. The story did not end there, though, for the Manus brothers. Although Irvine Manus lived, his life was not without peril. Later, *The Berea Citizen* reported on July 12, 1906 that Irvine Manus and Ambrose Farthing got into a fight over a woman and that Irvine was shot. With more than eighty wounds to his body, he was listed as being in a "dangerous condition."

All of this relates back to Barnes Mountain because of the cave. After he took off from his father's house and went on the run, George Lunsford spent his brief time in hiding within that small cave on the mountain. In his sobriety, he surely had the opportunity to think about his actions and what they meant to him. No doubt, he was also thinking about the possible lynching he might receive should anyone manage to find him and get their hands on him before the sheriff did. It might even be possible that he figured time in the pen to be a better alternative, although we'll never really know.

What we *do* know is that several people have heard the shouts and cries of an angry, disturbed man coming from that cave. In his fear, anger, and possibly drunkenness did he leave a trace of his energy behind? Or does George Lunsford's spirit still haunt the last place in which he was a free man?

There is another haunted cave story that stems from Barnes Mountain as well. As a result of the story, the cave itself has taken on the name "the baby cave."

In this story, a family lived in an older house close to the cemetery. The particulars around the story vary, depending on who is telling it. All of the variations end in the same way, however: the death of an infant.

In this family there was a son and a daughter, but something wasn't quite right with the son.

Haunted Estill County

Although we can only speculate as to what happened, the daughter became pregnant and the widespread rumor was that the baby belonged to her brother. (Although in other variations of the story the baby also belonged to the father and sometimes to a rambler who came in and took advantage of her before leaving town.)

In order to straighten the situation out, when the baby was born the father of the family took his grandchild into the cave and smothered it in a barrel of feathers, leaving behind its still warm body. Even now if you wander into that cave at the right time of night, you can hear the muffled sounds of a baby's cry.

Abandoned house on HYW 52

The Devil's House

Every town has that one house that everyone knows about and is secretly afraid to enter, even though they might find themselves creeping in there on a dare. It's the house that everyone talks about and speculates over but few really understand why it's meant to be scary and nobody can remember how the stories started. Irvine's house is located in the Sandhill area and is known as "The Devil's House." But what happened there and what really goes on once you step inside those doors?

Haunted Estill County

The house itself is an old farm house snuggled on a small hill at the end of a road. Painted red and still in fairly good condition despite its age and emptiness, it's seem more than its fair share of the curious and thrill seekers over the years as young and old alike wander through its rooms, seeking the ghosts that are said to haunt it.

Sometimes the rooms are freezing cold in the middle of summer–enough to make you want to wrap your arms around yourself. Other times, the rooms are so blazingly hot in the wintertime that you could swear the heater was turned on high, despite the fact nobody has lived in the house for a long, long time.

The house's inhabitants are not always the friendly kind of apparitions, either. Visitors have reported feeling pinched, tugged at, slapped, and one young thrill seeker claimed that he felt as though he was being stretched by both his arms and his legs when he walked inside.

Haunted Estill County

At one point, the walls inside boasted signs of Satanic activity with scribbles of Satan's name, disturbing symbols, and other sinister images. In fact, this is one of the reasons the house is called The Devil's House. Some believe that it is not only a doorway to Hell itself but that religious cults have practiced their rituals and spell work here over the years.

While the experiences inside might be enough to spook the most hardened non-believer, it's what follows you once you return home that might be even scarier, for whatever haunts The Devil's House is said to remain with those souls it takes a liking to.

Although many people have been able to tell me stories about The Devil's House, not everyone seems to be able to agree as to where it is located. Some say it's on Trotting Ridge. Others say Drowning Creek. One thing is for sure, however: visiting it might be an experience that you don't ever forget.

Haunted Estill County

The "Devil's House"

One of the big reasons why The Devil's House is such a fascinating place is due to the fact that it became a popular story in Estill County during the time when stories about devil worshipping and satanic rituals were so widespread. The 1980s saw a huge surge in devil worshipping hysteria. There were several factors in this and nobody can accurately trace its roots. I, myself, read a book called *Michelle Remembers* that was popular in the 1980s. It was about a woman who, through regression therapy, recalled her forgotten childhood and how she was forced to partake in satanic rituals and even fought with Lucifer himself. That spurred the popularity of trans-regressive therapy and might have been one of the jumping off points to what later became known as the "devil worshipping hysteria." For the record, the book itself was debunked. Michelle almost certainly made up the entire thing, although whether she purposefully lied or "saw" the memories through poor hypnosis and thought she was telling the truth might not ever be known.

In 1988, *The Kentucky New Era* ran a headline that stated "Devil Worship rumors rampant in portions of Eastern Kentucky." The article itself talks about police officers who were genuinely confused at the time by the large number of calls they were receiving from panicked residents who were certain that devil worshippers were practicing nearby or targeting them. A deputy with the Laurel County Sheriff's Department said that it was the first time that a rumor of that nature had grown to that proportion.

There were lots of different variations of the stories going around. Some said that Satanists were posing as vacuum cleaner salesmen. (It sure didn't seem to hurt the Rainbo sales at the time, though!) Other rumors were that the Satanists had to collect a certain number of children before Halloween so they could use them in a ritual. There was never any supporting evidence of any of this.

The devil worshipping hysteria directly affected Irvine in more ways than one. None of the stories are as torrid, however, as the incident that happened to Janice Braverman.

Janice was in Irvine as an artist-in-residence for one year under the Kentucky Arts Council. A Cincinnati photographer, she was approached by several teenage girls in the high school bathroom and was subsequently asked to take pictures of them. They were skipping class but when she talked to them about her photography project they acted interested. These were the kinds of students that she was interested in– those who might get easily discouraged in school and needed a creative outlet. After snapping a few shots, she showed them how to work her camera. Braverman was five feet tall and a fairly regular looking thirty-six year old woman. She did not dress in Goth style clothes, have wild hair, or (by her own words) have "jaggy eyebrows or long fingernails."

Unfortunately for her, the rumors of satanic cults looking for blond haired, blue eyed children for their rituals had hit Estill County at about the same time that she came to town. When word got out that a stranger had taken pictures of the local girls, stories began circulating that she was looking for potential victims for the satanic rituals. The school principal at the time refused to talk to her and even threatened to have her arrested when she went in to talk to him. Rumors were that he chased her out of the building, yelling at her to "get out."

Janice figured that she was the target of the rumors because she was from out of town and told the Associated Press that she had "never seen such hysteria over nothing." She also said the people who were accusing her, including the school's principal, never really took the time to get to know the real story and jumped to conclusions. She even compared the incident to the Salem witch trials and said that she finally understood how such a thing could have happened then since it was happening to her *now*.

Janice had to quickly leave Estill County under the fear that something might happen to her should she continue to hang around. Shaken, she was unsure whether or not she would even return to teaching again. She referred to the incident as a "nightmare."

There were other rumors at the time regarding devil worshipping that spread throughout the state. In

Haunted Estill County

Breathitt County, there were six people arrested after the Jackson police said that a grave robbery was linked to devil worshipping. A trailer the defendants were using was found with drawings of pentagrams and the words "Satan Rules." In Caldwell County, a mass panic occurred when almost half of all the students in the district left school when stories spread that devil worshippers were going to massacre the students.

To this day, nobody is really sure where these rumors got their origins. Many people in the county, today, believe that Janice Braverman was the product of overactive imaginations and officials that might not have handled the situation in the most productive manner. She does continue to be a well-respected photographer, however, and has continued her creative endeavors.

Dark Hollow Road

There are some roads that are so aptly named that it's impossible not to think there's something supernatural going on down them. Dark Hollow Road is one of these roads. The name itself lends itself to mystery, ghosts, and the paranormal.

The road is actually an innocuous one, despite its name, that runs off of HWY 52 right through Irvine's most populous business districts. The sign that marks the road is obvious and perches proudly on a corner that isn't too far from the county's only McDonalds.

Haunted Estill County

There is nothing menacing about the way it dips down and heads off to the countryside; indeed, it could very well be the opening to a subdivision. Still, those who have lived there in the past have spoken of specters and shadowy figures that hearken back to times long ago.

It was twilight as Mary Estep was driving home one evening. The sun had dipped down behind the mountains but there was still enough light on this spring day to illuminate the houses and trees as she drove by. Her house wasn't very far from HWY 52 and she was glad to be retiring to it after a long day of working in Richmond.

Lost in her daydreams, she nearly spun off the road when a woman stepped out in front of her car. Slamming on her brakes, she came to a screeching halt, making the little Camaro do a 180 degree spin until it came to a stop. Frightened, she jumped out, sure that she must have hit the young woman who had come from out of nowhere.

Haunted Estill County

When she looked around, however, the woman was gone. There was no sign of the glimpse of blond hair she had caught out of the corner or her eye that had almost cost her a damaged vehicle. There were no houses and few trees on this part of the road. The woman couldn't have gotten away that quickly.

A middle-aged couple was also driving home one evening and was almost to the end of the road when the woman noticed a young female standing off to the side. She appeared to be in distressed so the woman asked her husband to slow down. She was alone, after all, and although they were wary of picking up hitchhikers, she might have had car trouble and needed a call for a tow truck.

Both were confused, however, as they got a better look at the woman. She was indeed in distress, they could tell that by the way she was sobbing, but her clothing was very much outdated and in a style the man and woman had only seen in movies. She looked as if she had stepped out of "Little House on the Prairie" with her long calico dress, her high boots with laces, and her bonnet.

What was even more mystifying, however, was the way the evening light seemed to go *through* her instead of around her. "She's got a baby," the man exclaimed. The woman hadn't seen the bundle held tightly in the young woman's arm for the baby it was, but now that she did she found herself clutching the door handle, ready to jump out. She might have hesitated in helping a single person, but not someone with a child.

Almost as soon as she stepped out of the car, however, the woman and the baby simply disappeared. They didn't go away in a cloud of smoke or fade away: one moment they were there and the next moment they weren't.

Haunted Estill County

The woman in the bonnet has been seen on several occasions on Dark Hollow Road. Sometimes she appears with her baby and sometimes she doesn't have it and is seen wandering alone, in search of something.

She isn't the only apparition spotted on this stretch of road, however. One family rented a house on Dark Hollow Road for awhile and was visited by a ghostly presence on more than one occasion. The house was the site of a suicide; a man had shot himself on the front porch. There were some nights the sounds of heavy footsteps were so loud on the front porch the parents would have to get up and check on their children, sure that it was one of them traipsing around in the middle of the night. Of course, there was never anyone there.

The Black Dog of Death

Late in publication, a friend asked me about the mysterious black dog that members of her family had seen and wondered if I'd heard any other stories about it. At the time, I had not heard any other Estill Countian mention the black dog, but it was not an unfamiliar story to me. Over the course of the next few days, I asked around and was a little surprised to learn that it had been spotted by several people over the years. So what is this black dog and what does seeing it really mean? Let's start with the stories… Names, of course, have been changed.

Haunted Estill County

Mr. and Mrs. Bowman were lying in their bed one night, just about to fall asleep, when suddenly Mr. Bowman shot up and asked his wife if she had left the door open. She was confused by the terrified look on his face and immediately asked him what was wrong. He answered by asking her how a black dog had gotten inside their house. Concerned, she peered over the bed but as soon as she looked in its general direction, the dog quickly disappeared as though it had never been there to start with.

Although that experience was disturbing, it's not the only unusual disturbance that happened that very night. Mr. and Mrs. Bowman talked about the incident and decided that he must have been dreaming and still partly asleep when he had imagined it in their bedroom. They could not understand, however, how their son saw the same dog later that night.

Greg Bowman was walking his cousin home

when she glanced down and saw a large, black dog with dark brown eyes and just the slightest hint of red tingeing them walking alongside Greg. The dog would occasionally glance up at Greg, as though Greg was his master. However, when she mentioned the dog to him and he looked down, the dog disappeared, just as it had done in his parents' bedroom.

Like the shadow people, the black dog has been spotted throughout the county and doesn't seem to favor a particular place or time. It has been seen in the early morning hours, late at night, and in the middle of the afternoon. Sometimes it's been spotted inside a house where the owners had no such canines and other times it's been seen walking along the sidewalk, seemingly with a particular person, although when that person has looked down the dog disappears. He is almost always the same height (tall), the same color (black), and has the same kind of eyes (dark brown with tints of red). Some people report seeing a dog with shaggy hair, like a Golden Retriever. What Jennifer Andrews saw was more of a Labrador type.

Jennifer was visiting a cousin on Kissey Branch. She was not from the area but had spent a lot of time there when she was growing up. This happened to be summertime and they were getting up early to pick tomatoes. It had been excruciatingly hot for the past few days and they thought they might be able to beat the heat if they could get started early enough and retire before lunch, before heading back out again in the evening.

Rising at an uncharacteristically early hour, Jennifer was surprised to find that she was the first one up and outside. She used the time to take a stroll around the property and visit the barn where she had played as a child. Suddenly, however, she got the distinct feeling that something or someone was watching her. Turning, she expected to find her cousin standing before her, but was taken aback to see a large black dog. It sparkled in the early morning dew and stood stoic, staring at her with its head tilted to the side. She had always been an animal lover but something about this dog wasn't right. It had come from out of nowhere, for starters, and it had the reddest eyes she had ever seen.

Ordinarily, Jennifer would have tried to make friends with such a creature or at least acknowledge it and move on. This time, she did neither. Instead, she quickly turned and began walking away, heading back toward the house. After about ten feet, she turned and looked over her shoulder and was frightened to find the dog was just feet away from her. He was following her silently, yet made no sound when he moved.

Her instincts were to run. She so badly wanted to pick up her tennis-shoed feet and take off for the house, but she couldn't. Something told her that this dog was unique and that running might set off something inside of him that made him yearn for a chase and a kill. The hair on her arms and head stood up at point and chills ran down her neck as she purposefully walked toward the little stream by the barn. She wasn't sure why, but the stream looked inviting and she honestly felt that if she could make it to the other side the dog wouldn't follow her.

Each second she walked felt like an hour. She had never been so aware of a presence. Its eyes seemed to bore into her soul and probe at her as if trying to dislodge the secrets in her heart. With one last gasp, she hurled herself across the stream making a leap that she had never been able to manage in the past. When she looked back, the dog was gone. Her cousin, however, stood a few yards away. She hadn't even noticed him.

"Did you see that dog?" she asked as she scurried up the bank and ran to his side.

"I didn't see a dog," he answered. "But it looked like you were escaping from the gates of hell.

So what is this mysterious black dog?

The black dog, sometimes known as the "black dog of death", has been around for a long time and can be found in folk stories that go back to the British Isles and even Germany. He is known by many names and these can include the hellhound, Barghest, Galleytrot, the Yelp Hound, Padfoot, Shuck, Snarleyow, Striker, Trash, Wish or Whist Hound, or even a pooka. (Although, to be fair, the pooka is normally considered a benign being and is not associated with anything malevolent.)

The black dog is usually thought to be an omen of sorts. Sometimes his presence is followed shortly by a run of bad luck or even the death of a close friend or family member. Although in the folktales it was almost sudden and sure death to touch one, they are not supposed to be physical manifestations at all and are, instead, preternatural. Some stories claim the black dog

Haunted Estill County

is actually a mischievous spirit, out to cause mischief but no real harm. Other stories have him as the physical manifestation of the devil himself.

The fact is, though, his presence is seen all over the world and has been described in much the same way by people who have never met one another or have any reason to tell a similar sounding story. He shows up near bodies of water, on streets, and in graveyards. He can be seen inside and out.

A Haunting in Pryse

Ravenna was originally built as a railroad town and the river was once used to float logs to Frankfort. As a result, many small communities built up along the train tracks and near the water. Over the years, those communities like Miller's Creek, Pryse, and even Hargett (nothing left now but the store and a few churches) have mostly disappeared and now all that's left are a few houses with hardly a reminder there were once stores, businesses, and entire families that made the place their home.

One such community is located near the edge of Estill County. At one time it was a budding village, complete with stores and shops. Today, those are all closed and only a couple of abandoned structures even hint at the community's past. Nearby, an abandoned oil field is forlorn and overgrown.

The "shadow being" is common in the paranormal world and many have their ideas as to what this entity is. Although these shadow people have been seen all over the county, this one seems to be anchored to this particular house. No matter what your interpretation of this black, shadowy, human-like form might be, most people who have seen it think it's alive and well at the big house in this lonesome valley. Feeling far removed from the rest of the county, there is something eerie about a community that has all but vanished, leaving nothing behind but farms and fields and one of the most beautiful houses in the county.

Before you venture too far into this house, however, you might want to take caution. Even when the house has been empty, faces peering out of the windows have been detected.

For those who have lived in the house, the stories just get stranger. On warm, summer evenings the unmistakable chill in the air seems to be far more than just the draft of an old house. In fact, the word "freezing" is often used to describe the temperature on days that should have been hot and humid. And, as you wander through the rooms, the feel of eyes may follow you with each step, which is enough to leave anyone feeling a little spooked.

It is the shadow being that wants to follow visitors throughout the rooms, however, that might be the most disconcerting. Disappearing as quickly as it appeared, it is ever watchful and vigilant. What does it want? What *is* it?

Haunted Estill County

As communities started dissipating and families left farming and no longer depended on the river as much, the towns got bigger. The hamlets suffered. Is the house on this valley floor haunted by a demon, the devil, or merely a sad memory of days gone by?

The Oil Boom Murders

Estill County has seen a lot of industries come and go over the years. The furnaces were a major draw for many years. They brought in workers from all over the country and entire communities were built around the profession. Those communities are almost completely gone today. The trees of Estill County were also a draw for a long time as lumber yards cut them down and sent them to the river where they were used elsewhere in the state. Then, of course, there is the town of Ravenna which was built by the railroad. We can't forget Estill Springs, either; a large resort that saw visitors from not just all over the state but all over the south. And, in a time when nearly every community in the United States was suffering, Carhartt opened a plant here during the Great Depression. These are all stories that we hear about quite a lot. The history of the oil boom, however, is a quiet one. The murders that happened during that time are almost unheard of.

"There's oil in them thar hills," you can almost hear someone shouting. There is, indeed, oil in Estill County, and although it may never be the hotbed for oil drilling that Texas and Alaska are, some people have benefited quite well from the black water that runs under our mountains. Pryse Road had an entire community built for the oil boom. You can still see the drums and carcasses from that time period, although the gates are locked and it's all abandoned now. There was another area, too, that yielded a substantial amount of oil and still does. It was closer to the Powell County line. That is where this story takes place.

When a community starts booming in business, others flock to it looking for work. There is usually not enough housing available for those who are seeking it. For that reason, other businesses pop up as well- boarding houses, hotels, campgrounds, etc.

This particular house was used for that sole reason: to house the workers who came for the oil.

The woman who ran the boarding house was a smart one. She knew that she needed money and she knew that others would be looking for a place to stay. She could provide room and board for a modest fee and the workers could stay close to their jobs.

Everyone benefited from the arrangement. Well, that is, everyone benefited until folks started turning up dead.

Nobody will probably ever know why she killed the boarders. Perhaps it was self-defense. Perhaps it was an accident. Perhaps they found out something about her that she didn't want others to know. Or, perhaps she was just crazy. At any rate, more than boarder died by her hands. Their bodies she cast away in the sinkholes that dotted her property.

Folks who have visited the house have spoken of hearing the sounds of screaming, loud thuds in the night, and footsteps running up and down the floorboards. Is someone still trying to escape the house? Are there spirits still trapped within those walls, trying to seek their final resting place but unable to get out? Some say you can still see a stain on the steps where a man was killed and left to suffocate on his own blood.

Haunted Estill County

A walk in these hills is a quiet one. There are few houses and even fewer people out on even a pretty, warm day. Sounds echo, though, and a stranger might not be able to tell where they are originating from. The cries and the moans are disturbing enough, but sometimes the stillness is even more chilling. Is there still something evil waiting in these woods where the oil is drilled?

Haunted Estill County

Restless Spirits

Not all spirits are dangerous, of course. Not all houses are haunted by just one ghost from one time period, either. Sometimes, a house can be a portal and allow in many ghosts and spirits who had nothing to do with the place in which they haunt. Is that true for the small house downtown off of Broadway in Irvine? We might never know but one thing we can say for certain: it is haunted by more than one person.

The house is a rental unit, although dwellers tend not to stay for very long. Built around 1940, it's a small two bedroom house with a single bathroom. At less than 1,000 square feet, it is not an imposing structure. Friendly and inviting, it has the charm of many of the older homes in the area. It is in need of work, however, yet updates are hard to come by. Why? Because the spirits apparently don't want any work done to it.

A benign spirit, the most commonly seen apparition is that of a little girl. She's unobtrusive yet curious and can often be heard bouncing her ball around the house. Sounds are particularly loud coming from the attic area. Those who have spent the night in the house have claimed to have heard her laughing and singing, although they can't say what song it was–only that it sounded like an older one.

Another spirit is that of an old man. Also benevolent, he has a protective nature about him since he checks in on the children who are sleeping there every morning before he turns and goes out through the back door.

Then, there is the spirit of the young man. His clothing changes from time to time. Sometimes he is wearing tan pants and a white shirt. Other times he's wearing dark colored pants and a light colored shirt. What doesn't change, however, is the fact that he loves the modern appliances the house has. He can be seen standing over the washing machine, the oven, and the toaster…just watching.

While these spirits seem to be harmless, they aren't always passive. There are reports of people being pushed down, objects flying into the dweller's face, and loud noises that go on all night making it impossible for anyone to get any sleep.

Another house not too far away is also home to wandering and restless spirits.

In this house, voices can be heard every morning. The rising sounds of a couple arguing are often overshadowed by their stomping footsteps as they march from room to room in anger.

These spirits, unlike some, seemed to be able to move things at their will, too. Doors left open will suddenly close. Cabinet doors fly open on their own. When people call in on the house phone, they often report hearing heavy breathing and other sounds. Once, the dweller was even pushed so hard in her living room that she was injured and had to seek hospital care.

So who are these ghosts and what did they want? Are they angry that someone is living in their home? Are they merely reenacting scenes from their lives? If so, are the living like ghosts to the spirits themselves–unwanted visitors who are trespassing in their house?

Many people have taken photographs, only to look at them later and see images that were not present when they were actually taking the photos. This can be chalked up to double exposures or errors in the cameras. Other times, however, there are no explanations–at least not any explanations not grounded in the supernatural.

When Emma and Rick rented the small house in Ravenna they had no reason to be afraid of it. They hadn't heard any stories about the house itself, had met at least one of the previous renters, and the house really wasn't that old to begin with.

The renters never heard any strange noises, were never disturbed in their sleep, and never saw any odd shadows or people who weren't supposed to be there. However, they *did* have a problem with their photographs: Every time a picture was taken inside the home, it would be full of disbelieving images. Sometimes there would be orbs floating around the body of their youngest daughter. Other times, the very plain image of an old woman would seem to hover in the background. In some photos, it would be the image of an old man.

They did their research and did not uncover any deaths in the home. Indeed, the same couple had owned the home since it was built and were very much alive and living out of state. So who were the spirits that kept showing up in the photographs and what did they want?

When a house catches on fire, the whole thing doesn't always burn down and it's simple enough to patch up the parts that are left. That's what happened in this mid-century home in Irvine.

During the 1950s, part of the house caught on fire, taking the lives of the man who lived there and his young son. Although the house was repaired and even built onto later, the house apparently remembers the tragedy that befell it more than fifty years ago.

The young boy who perished in the fire is still

very much a part of the house and the land around it. Those who have lived there have reported seeing his spirit passing from room to room and even throwing things around as he attempts to play in his afterlife. Balls have been heard bouncing on the floors, small rocks have been thrown at unsuspecting people, and the sound of laughter can be heard throughout the house in the early morning hours.

The other two spirits who haunt the house are not so benign, however. A disheveled woman was reported searching through the house and yard at a frantic speed and has been known to slam doors and cause sleep disturbances. A middle aged man can be heard stomping and screaming and the sounds are often followed by the young boy's cry, leading some to wonder if he didn't harm the boy intentionally before the house caught fire.

There have even been times when the house has been known to scream. The current owners wonder if

Haunted Estill County

perhaps the young boy was abused or hurt.

Although the man's spirit has apparently passed on, the young boy continues to haunt the walls in which he died.

Haunted Estill County

Trotting Ridge Cemetery

Cemeteries are prime locations for ghosts and restless spirits and I think you would probably find that most of the cemeteries in Estill County have ghost stories attached to them. The following two stories, however, are about a cemetery close to Trotting Ridge.

When Lisa and her friends were in high school they drove to the cemetery to park and smoke and drink some of the whiskey that had been taken from one of the girls' houses. However, after being there for a few minutes, Lisa got the strangest feeling that someone was watching them. When she looked out her window, a young man dressed in old fashioned clothes was leaning against a fence post, staring in their direction.

At first, she thought that another car might have pulled up or that someone had wandered over from a neighboring house to see what they were up to. The longer she looked at the man, however, the more convinced she became that he was not human. For one thing, there weren't any stars in the night sky and the moon was hidden behind a cloud yet he had the strangest, most ethereal glow about him. Then there was the fact that nothing about his clothing appeared modern.

As she continued to watch him, he vanished.

In another similar circumstance, Jonathan and two of his friends decided to go on a ghost hunt around the cemetery after hearing others talk about its spookiness. Hoping to catch a glimpse of a ghost they came armed with cameras and flashlights.

Haunted Estill County

After wandering around for about fifteen minutes they were just about ready to give up when one of them caught something out of the corner of his eye. Motioning to the others, they turned and were surprised to see a man dressed in old fashioned clothes and an old, large brimmed, farmer's hat walking up the gravel road.

Thinking that it was someone coming to run them off, they started toward the man, ready with explanations and apologies. To their surprise, however, the man disappeared right in front of them. All three of the boys, now grown men, were able to describe him in minute detail, even though it was a moonless night and they shouldn't have been able to see that far ahead of them.

The Big Cats

According to many biologists, there are no large cats in Eastern Kentucky. And by "large cats" I don't mean the occasional twenty pound tabby; I am talking about mountain lions and pumas. Supposedly, mountain lions have been gone from the area since the early 1920s and pumas were never here to begin with. However, many residents would beg to differ and have the pictures to prove it.

For many years now sightings of a large, black, panther-like creature have been seen throughout the region. Not just your regular over-fed cat, this guy is about four feet long with an estimated weight of close to two-hundred pounds. He has been spotted at least three times in Estill County, including by Lock 12, at the landfill, and on a farm on Wagersville Road.

Cryptology is an interesting part of the paranormal world and there are enthusiasts out there with websites dedicated to finding and proving the existence of this mysterious black cat. What is he and where did he come from? Some of those who haven't seen him still talk about hearing screams in the night that sound as if they are coming from a woman or a small child. Some have woken up the next morning to find their goats and even their cows slashed with claw marks.

Others have seen glimpses of long black tails, nearly a yard long in some instances, as they whip around the corners of their houses and barns. One woman woke up one morning after a snow and saw large paw prints and a tail print dragging behind. The tail print itself was nearly two feet long, much too long to have belonged to a house cat.

There is no reasonable explanation for these creatures. Kentucky was never known for having black panthers. As with many things ostensibly improvable, however, that doesn't mean they don't exist.

The Drowning Creek Ambush

In my research I have found that very few of the "back stories", so to speak, can be proven with simple research. Most are stories that have been passed down from person to person and, as stories go, they change a little bit with every passing. There is one, however, that *is* provable and unfortunately it has to be one of the saddest that I have encountered.

Several sources talk about visiting a small, veritably unmarked, cemetery off of Drowning Creek. It's a point that overlooks the water and takes a little bit of hiking to get to. It's off the beaten path and not somewhere you can wander around without first knowing where it is and also getting permission (or at least be prepared to answer some questions).

The stories all have their own details and fine points but one thing remains the same: soldiers haunt the grounds. Sometimes the soldiers appear to be shooting back. Other times the soldiers are laughing and talking. They are always dressed in their uniforms, however, and appear tired, worn. They are young men, probably in their late twenties or early thirties. Some of the stories have omitted the soldiers all together but include other details.

When John was walking around the graves with his grandfather one night in the middle of October they were struck by the sound of guns. At first they thought that someone on a nearby farm might be shooting at coyotes or something that was bothering their animals. The sounds were hollow, however, and when they came again they sounded so close that both men dropped to the ground. For nearly ten seconds it sounded as if the guns were firing around them, surrounding them on all sides. Then it was over.

With trepidation, both men stood and looked around, using their flashlights. The shots were so close the people firing them must have only been a few feet away. There was nobody around, however. Later they would describe the gunfire and admit that as close as it sounded, something felt "off" about it, like it was something they were hearing from a television set. Except, of course, there were no television sets anywhere near them.

In a similar story, Eric talks about the time he was walking close to the graveyard and saw a young man running through the field. He was dressed in period clothing and kept looking over his shoulder as if in fear. At first, not realizing what he was seeing, Eric took off after him. It was only after he got within several feet of him the soldier disappeared, the look of terror still on his face.

Haunted Estill County

So who are these soldiers, why are they running, and what is the gunfire that can sometimes be heard?

Samuel Allen, from Virginia, married Susan Sizemore. Together, they had seven sons: Andrew, Irvine (or Ervine) James, George, John, Ira, and Emory. They were all born in the 1830s and 1840s. When the Civil War began, all seven joined the Confederacy. Almost all of them attained rank.

As we know, Kentucky was literally split in half during the Civil War: brothers fought against brothers and cousins against cousins. There was no clear line dividing the north and the south in our state. Unfortunately, not everything went back to the way it was after the war. Bad feelings died hard.

James, Andrew, and Ira were all killed in battle. The war ended, however, and the rest of the sons were given train tickets back to either Louisville or Lexington and were happily on their way home in August of 1865 when even more tragedy struck. John Alfred, Emory,

Haunted Estill County

and Irvine Allen were ambushed by a group of Union soldiers at the mouth of Drowning Creek here in Estill County. Despite the fact they had all sworn their oath to the Union, they were all murdered, along with their friends Drew (Drury) Fletcher Gwinn and David Richardson, by Yankee Home Guards. George was the only surviving son to return back home. Children, widows, and grieving parents were left behind.

Gabriel's Trumpet

Starting around 2008, tales of mysterious sounds began making their way across the globe. Those who have heard it have called it "indescribable" but likened it to the sound of a huge brass instrument blaring out a note. Others have found that although they can hear it plainly, not everyone around them can even hear it at all. It comes at different intervals and without warning. Around 2012, the noise was heard in Irvine by several of the residents. So what is this strange sound and what does it mean?

Some are convinced that it's a sign of alien aircraft hovering in the Earth's atmosphere. It must be an invisible one since something that large would not go unnoticed.

Others are convinced the sounds are part of a government experiment and local people point toward the Bluegrass Army Depot which, probably fairly in most cases, gets blamed for a lot of the unusual activity in the area.

Still, there are others who strongly believe the sound is that of Gabriel blowing his trumpet, a sure sign that the apocalypse is coming.

When Marvin Anderson first heard the sound close to Hargett he thought another gas line had exploded. A few minutes later, he was sure his ears were playing tricks on him and that it was merely a train; a loud one, but a train nevertheless. The sound was a sad one and sent chills down his spine. What was unusual about this sound, aside from the fact that there weren't any trains going by, was rather than coming from one single direction the sound seemed to come from everywhere. It took over the air around him and became just as much a part of it as the heat on that July morning. Even the birds stopped singing. For the five minutes that he estimated the sound continued, he didn't want to do anything but sit down and cry.

Emily Richardson heard a similar sound a few months later on the other side of the county on Wagersville Road. Working in her garden one afternoon, she thought at first that it might be the emergency alert system having trouble with its speakers. There were no clouds in the sky and no sign of an oncoming store so the noise confused her. As she continued to listen, however, the noise started sounded less like static and more like music. She describes it as one long, continuous, note being blasted by a large brass instrument. It wasn't unpleasant to her ears, but there was something melancholy and eerie about it. Her dog became so frightened that he ran under the porch and it took her more than an hour to coax him back out. Even the cows and horses in the fields stopped and stared at the sky, questioningly.

People all over the world are reporting hearing similar noises. They have described the sounds as drumming, squeaking, blaring, and roaring. Although the descriptions might vary, the general consensus does not: the sounds are coming from the sky.

In various religions, the sound of horns has been used to signify radical change. Gabriel is the one spoken of in the Book of Revelation who blows the final trumpet announcing Judgment Day (Rev. 11:15). Although Gabriel blaring his trumpet is prevalent in Christianity as the start of revelations, it's not the only religion to talk about such things. Even the ancient religions that predate Christianity have such myths.

The noises have been recorded and a simple

search will allow you to listen to them yourself. But what are these noises? Some scientists say they are electromagnetic waves. Others think they are "sky quakes." The fact is, there may or may not be any reasonable explanation for them. At this time, nobody knows for sure.

Unsolved Murders

When a county has been around for more than one hundred years it's going to have its fair share of unsolved murders. Estill County is no different in this aspect. What is unusual, in some cases, though, is that despite the small size of the county the murders themselves have been very mysterious. Not only are they unsolved, in some cases they're downright intriguing.

In the early years, it was relatively easy to commit a crime and get by scott-free. The forensics of the time were nothing like they are today. In fact, fingerprinting itself is a relatively modern idea. Still, in the later years, getting by with murder took a lot more skill (and probably even more luck). Although the following is not a complete list of some of the county's biggest unsolved murder cases, they do represent a few of the most well-known.

The Daisy Horn Case

In early January of 1930, the body of Daisy Horn was discovered close to the east end of the South Irvine Bridge. She had at least three bullet wounds in her chest. Daisy was about nineteen years old and the daughter of Boyd (Void) and Minnie Horn, who lived near South Irvine.

Just a day before her murder, young Ferrell Lewis was sworn in as coroner. He just completed his training and was new to the job and the business. Later, he and his brother would open the Lewis Funeral Home.

Haunted Estill County

On the morning that he took office, Daisy's murder occurred. It was quite a first case for this young man. Her body had been found by her neighbors right after the swearing-in ceremonies.

Daisy was young and likable and had just spent the week entertaining her brother who was in from out of town. Before she left that evening she had told her mother that she was going to meet someone. She didn't say who that person was.

Ferrell Lewis called in medical personnel to look at her young, bullet-ridden body. A pistol had been fired at her three times, with one bullet lodging in her arm and the other two hitting her in the chest, killing her. Her body was not something the young coroner would forget for some time.

When questioned, Daisy's mother told the police that Daisy's friend, Ancil Profitt, visited her on the night that she was killed. He was consequently arrested and brought to court the same day on suspicion of murder. This was not his first run-in with the law. In fact, just a year prior to Daisy's murder he had been convicted of making moonshine and had gotten into other scrapes along the way. He was no stranger to the justice system in Estill County.

Many people crowded into the courtroom to hear the proceedings, as the community was outraged over young Daisy's seemingly senseless death. Three witnesses took the stand and testified that they heard Profitt say if she ever dated anyone else he would kill her. The flaw in the prosecution, however, came when he swore he was eating supper in the Broadway Café at the same time of the murder. He had alibis that could put him there. In the end, there were never any charges brought against him.

There was a standstill in Daisy's murder case for five more years until another suspect, Shade Ingram, with an extensive criminal record was indicted for her murder. However, he wasn't convicted, either.

Farcilla (Fairalie) Reece

About a year later, in May of 1931, another mysterious murder occurred when the body of twenty year old Farcilla Reece was discovered in her room in South Irvine. She had been shot through the heart.

On the morning of May, 24, 1931, John Farrell was out for a walk. As he walked by a house, through a window he saw the body of a young woman, on a bed, covered by a coat. A local doctor owned the house and had rented it to a young woman by the name of Farcilla (or Fairalie) Reece. She had only been living there for a week.

When he walked by a little while later, he noticed that her body hadn't moved. Sensing that something might be wrong, he shouted and knocked on the door but couldn't stir her. The door was locked so he called the sheriff, C.C. Stanfill.

When the sheriff arrived, he was able to get inside the house where he discovered that Farcilla was deceased. It appeared that she'd been shot in the heart with a pistol at close range. There were powder burns on her breast. It was easy to rule out suicide since there wasn't a gun anywhere nearby.

She was given an autopsy and then placed in a make-shift coffin and buried at Doe Creek. There wasn't much hoopla around her burial and it was done very quickly.

Of course, an investigation had to be done regarding her death to find out who the murderer was. The sheriff learned that Farcilla had asked her neighbor, Mrs. Frank Dawes, to call a taxi for her on the night she was killed. Bev Harris was the taxi driver and had picked her up at about 7:00 PM. He had driven her to the Ravenna train station and during the car ride she asked him to inform M.V. Abston that she was going to

Haunted Estill County

Lee County. She claimed that she was going to testify in a moonshine case and wanted to visit her mother before going to court on Monday. M.V. Abston was forty-three years old and a wholesale grocery salesman from Lee County. He and Farcilla had been having an affair.

Once she got to the train station, she walked up to the Cruse Hotel and Restaurant. It was there that her trail ended for a little while. Although she left the restaurant for awhile, she accidentally left her hatbox behind and returned around 11:00 pm to pick it back up. Jim Fielder, who was standing in front of the hotel, watched her get into a car and leave with a man. He later said that he thought the man was Abston. That was the last time Farcilla was seen alive.

Later evidence showed that not only had Abston arranged to have her place in Irvine rented for her but that he had arranged her previous residence as well. It was established, too, that during the time in which she had disappeared from the restaurant, before returning to get her hatbox, Abston had searched for her. John Worrell, who was working at the train depot, said that Abston had come by looking for Farcilla. In fact, he seemed very interested in knowing where the hatbox was. He had also visited Coleman Gilbert's house on Cow Creek, trying to find her.

Abston was indicted and tried for her murder. Ezart Ashcraft and a team of Lee County attorneys defended him. Although he admitted his relationship with Farcilla, he denied any wrongdoing in regards to her demise. Abston claimed that during the night of her murder he'd suffered from stomach problems and had gone to bed in his room at the Cruse Hotel and hadn't woken up until the next day. Despite the fact the prosecution had more than thirty witnesses and a seemingly strong case, the jury found him not guilty.

About a year after the murder, Abston died of a heart attack. Of course, there were many questions that remained after her death. What was in the hatbox that was so important to Abston? Where did she disappear to when she left the restaurant? And did her involvement in the moonshine case have anything to do with her untimely death?

The Dave Woolery Case

The 1930s were a time of economic depression and hardships for everyone. Although Estill County survived better than some counties, especially thanks to the relocation of the Carhartt factory, it didn't completely scrape by without incident.

On March 8, 1931, thirty-three year old Dave Woolery was discovered hanging in the barn of R. M. Garrett at White Oak. He had gone to Irvine to pick up his paycheck and buy groceries on Saturday and seemed to be in a good mood at that time. He had just bought a farm and appeared to be looking forward to getting settled on it.

Sometime later, he walked to Mr. Garrett's house to get a tire from the barn. Garrett was his neighbor, as well as his boss. He saw Dave go into his barn but didn't see him come back out. The matter left his mind until the next morning when Dave's body was found, hanging from the rafters, by a chain. There was a red bandanna tied around his neck.

When the authorities arrived on the scene they determined the case a suicide. However, everyone who knew Dave was very surprised that a man who seemed to so happy would kill himself.

Conducting an investigation would have been difficult, though, since there was a lot of mud in the barn and it seemed obvious the poor fellow had hung himself. It was quickly decided that he had placed the bandana around his neck, put the chain around that, and then jumped from the loft.

He was quickly buried and the matter was

closed. Well, it was officially closed. It was not forgotten by his widowed wife and their eight year old daughter. Nor was it forgotten by his brother.

Some things about Dave's death had bothered his brother from the start and these details continued to nag at him. Why would have buy a farm if he was just planning on killing himself? Was he really that depressed that nobody had noticed? Why was he smiling when they saw his face? But, perhaps more importantly, why wasn't there any mud on the bottom of Dave's shoes yet his shirtsleeves and hands were covered in it?

After some careful consideration, the family asked for an official autopsy. The body was brought back up and an examination was performed, revealing that his neck wasn't broken and that he probably didn't die from the hanging.

Now, everyone truly believed that he had been killed somewhere else and then taken to the barn. He was probably dragged which explained why his feet didn't have mud on them, but his shirt did. The hanging was intended to look like a suicide.

It was still confusing, however. Who killed Dave Woolery? Speculations flew. Some said that his wife, Rosa, had been out riding with Taylor Sparks (a local farmer) and another man and woman the night before Dave was murdered. Rumors of their affair abounded. The new speculation was that Rosa and the two men murdered her husband.

The suspicions continued to mount until the three were indicted on May 13, 1938. This was more than seven years after the alleged murder. However, before Taylor Sparks could be tried, J. D. Puckett, a relative of Woolery's, shot him to death in September of 1938. He left behind a wife and several children. In February 1939, Rosa Woolery and Zack Walden were convicted and sentenced to life in jail. The prosecution argued that Rosa and the two men planned his death and then drugged and murdered him.

The mysterious events were not over yet, in this case, though. Both verdicts were later overturned by the Court of Appeals which ruled there was insufficient evidence for a guilty verdict. J. D. Puckett was sentenced to ten years in prison for the slaying of Taylor Sparks. The murder of Dave Woolery is still considered unsolved.

The Bear Horn Case

The railroad tracks in Estill County have seen their share of tragedy. In fact, it isn't railroad accidents that seem to cause the most mayhem, but the murders that take place around the tracks. Something about them just seems to draw murder and mystery. More than one murder has been committed by the railroad and more than one of these murders is still listed as "unsolved."

Haunted Estill County

Near the mouth of Cow Creek, on July 4, 1939, Elmer "Bear" Horn was found decapitated on the railroad tracks. He was the twenty-five year old son of Clell and Viola Lynch Horn who lived near the top of Mt. Scratchum on the Cow Creek side of the mountain. A hard working couple, by all accounts, they supplemented their small income by selling eggs and milk in town. Since they lacked transportation they could be seen walking into town on occasion, carrying their items in saddlebags. Nobody had a bad word to say about the couple.

There were a few stories circulating about Bear at the time of his murder, however. He had lost his ear in a car accident and was known to drink excessively as a result. Some people thought he was almost always under the influence of whiskey. When he was found dead, most people assumed that he had been drinking and had fallen asleep on the tracks and been run over the train.

Haunted Estill County

The problem with this assumption was that there weren't any wounds on the body, other than the decapitation marks. It seemed unlikely a train could run over someone and not leave any marks, or at least throw his body off the tracks from the sheer force of its speed. Now, people started wondering if, perhaps, he was murdered and his body was placed on the tracks to look like an accident–or to be discovered.

Theories abounded and none of them proved to be true or untrue, as is often the case in unsolved murders. One of the most prevalent rumors was that Bear had gotten into an argument with a bootlegger who, along with his wife, had killed Bear with an ax. There is no proof to this story and no formal charges were ever brought forth. After his death, Clell had Bear's Model A Ford parked in a gully close to his house as a tribute to his son. For a long time passersby could see the vehicle, until it finally got covered up in silt and debris.

Loretta Willoughby

One of the most recent, and probably famous, unsolved murder cases involves a young girl who was really no more than a child. The case itself continues to be a hot topic of conversation in the county and one that has spurred many speculations and rumors. Although not everyone can agree on what happened, one thing that everyone can agree on is this: Loretta Willoughby's death deserves some sort of justice and closure.

Loretta Lynn Willoughby was just fifteen years old with a young child when she went missing in downtown Irvine. Most everyone who knew her has said that she was a quiet, sweet, and pretty girl. She was raising her young son and living just a couple of blocks from Main Street.

On the day of her disappearance, Loretta walked

to Main Street to a grocery store. She was last seen leaving the store. Witnesses say that she had her head down and walked as though something was on her mind.

Three months later, her body was found close to a popular path in the woods behind her house. The path was well-traveled so why it took three months to discover her body is not known. She had been brutally murdered.

There were several speculations as to who might have done the killing, but no one was ever charged. Before his death, local school bus driver Buster Rawlings claimed to have admitted to killing her and disposing of her body but it is not widely believed that this is true. Many people believe that Buster suffered from problems near the end of his life and might have made that confession in confusion.

To this day, efforts have been made to reopen the case and investigate into her death even further. A

Facebook page has been set up and a petition has gone around in an attempt to get her story on *America's Most Wanted*. Oddly enough, when her death is discussed on popular public websites, more often than not those discussions are removed not long after they begin. Did Loretta know something that she wasn't supposed to? Was she silenced for a reason? Or was she simply in the wrong place at the wrong time? Her death, which appears to be a crime of passion considering the details of the murder, is one that has stuck with many people for years.

Alex Richardson

Alexander (Elic or Alex) Richardson was born in 1873 to Levi Richardson and Armilda (Kirby) Richardson. Although not much is known about Alex's personal life and many of the details of the case have

Haunted Estill County

been lost to history, the murder he was "tried" for is really one of the saddest, and most heinous, crimes that Estill County has seen.

On October 7, 1894 Barbara White, a local resident, left her home and was walking to a nearby store. Presumably from out of nowhere, someone clubbed her and killed her. Records also indicate that she was raped, or at the very least sexually assaulted in the attack. At the same time as her murder, Alex was hunting rabbits. He appeared with blood on his clothing and was presumed to be the murderer. He was subsequently arrested and taken to the Estill County jail.

Before any kind of trial could take place, a lynch mob took him by force from the jail and he was hanged over the railroad bridge for the crime he supposedly committed.

Where the story gets murkier is when, on his death bed, Wiley White confessed to committing the

Haunted Estill County

murder of his wife himself. Whether this was the confession of a man finally clearing his conscience or the ramblings of a sick individual who didn't know what he was confessing to will never be known.

According to *The Noose and the Chair* by Robert Barker, "At one time there was a rumor afloat that Wylie White, who had moved to another state, confessed that he had killed his own wife, but this could not be authenticated."

Alex Richardson is buried in Kirby Cemetery. His tombstone reads: "A precious one from us is gone. A voice we loved is stilled. A place is vacant in our home. Which can never be filled. The innocent little dove."

Haunted Estill County

The Furnaces

You really can't write anything about Estill County without including something about the iron furnaces. The furnaces, which were once the county's biggest industry, have not been in operation in more than a century. Still, their remnants continue to stand, even if all other indications of their past have been removed. There is no sign, for instance, of the once thriving community of Fitchburg that once survived around Fitchburg Furnace. Those who have been to Cottage Furnace in recent years might have a hard time believing that it once drew tons of workers and Estill Steam Furnace is essentially no more than a large pile of stones at this point.

At one time, however, the furnaces roared and the industry was a busy one. While many people made their money off of the furnaces, and from the businesses the furnaces encouraged to grow alongside of them, others did not fare as well.

Cottage Furnace, especially, has had its share of stories.

Several people have reported hearing cries of pain and seeing ghostly figures of men running and screaming around the Cottage Furnace area. Others, while not seeing anything unusual, have reported feeling like something (or somebody) was watching them while they walked around. They talk about feeling claustrophobic and have trouble breathing the closer they get to the stones.

There are two sad stories that revolve around Cottage Furnace.

The first story involves a slave named Ned. The young man had apparently escaped from his owner, who was known for being very cruel and barbaric, and was running away from him. He found shelter with a scientist named Jesse who lived in Marbleyard and found a job at the furnace. He was doing well there when his owner found him and began chasing after him. Instead of letting himself be caught and taken back to the farm where he would assuredly be beaten (or worse) he flung himself into the fiery furnace and burned to death in the molten iron ore.

Haunted Estill County

The furnaces were almost outdated before they were even built. Fitchburg Furnace was constructed as a charcoal furnace even though a lot of the furnaces at the time were converting to coal. It closed in the Panic of 1873 when the speculation bubble broke and a short recession occurred.

On the other hand, Cottage Furnace closed in 1879 when the furnace's owner, Joel McKinney, learned that his son had died. Even though the furnace was operating in full blast, in his grief the owner had it quickly shut down. The iron ore solidified and blocked the furnace so that it was never usable again.

Not everyone has reported feeling anything amiss when visiting the furnaces. A few people, however, claim to hear the roaring of the furnace late at night when they venture close to Fitchburg.

Haunted Estill County

Bumps in the Night

When I started putting these stories together I was really searching for complete stories–tales with beginnings, middles, and ends. Not all hauntings have these, of course. Sometimes, and maybe even most of the time, we just don't know what's making those noises or why a place is haunted. A place doesn't have to have a violent past or a complicated tale to encourage a haunting. The haunting doesn't even have to be related to the house at all. Sometimes, it's the land, a piece of furniture, or even a person that's haunted.

So what about the haunted places in Estill

Haunted Estill County

County with other unexplained occurrences? The following is a short list of these locations and some of the bumps and thumps the former and current residents have heard...

The old house on Main Street that was once a funeral home: Reports of footsteps walking around on the second floor, the smell of cigar smoke coming on strongly when no one in the house is smoking, and doors opening and closing by themselves have all been shared in regards to this house.

The Poplar Street house: While there isn't a known reason for the haunting, residents and guests of this house on Poplar Street claim to feel their beds shaking in the night, the touch of hands that try to push them down the stairs, and .the ghostly image of otherworldly visitors who watch over them while they sleep.

Dry Branch Road: A woman and her son supposedly haunt a house on Dry Branch Road. They break glass and move things around.

Hargett School: The old Hargett school house has gotten a lot of attention for being haunted. There are supposedly multiple spirits haunting the grounds, although whether they're spirits, ghosts, demons, or shadow people is debatable.

The Wig Wam: Although there aren't any specific stories about the Wig Wam, one of the county's oldest running establishments, there are quite a few people who claim to get bad vibes from the building and don't feel comfortable going inside. Others don't have a problem with it and love their box meals.

Haunted Estill County

Ravenna grade school: No evidence or research, so far, supports this story, but apparently a little girl was murdered near the old Ravenna grade school. Now her little ghost haunts the grounds and the hallways.

The caves of Estill County: Estill County is home to several different cave systems and some of these are purportedly haunted. Tucker Cave and California Cave seem to have the most activity. Visitors have felt eyes watching them, heard footsteps and whispers, and seen shadow people while inside.

Lost love in Fox: Another unverifiable story, but a sad one, involves the Fox area of the county. When slavery was still going on in Kentucky, a family in nearby Madison County had a female slave while a family in Estill County had her love working for them. One day the young man was sold and was placed on a boat and sent down the river. His young love threw herself on the river banks and cried as his boat went past her. The ghost of this young woman has supposedly been spotted standing on the riverbanks, waiting for him to return.

Haney Hollow: At the foot of Barnes Mountain, a little boy was supposedly killed with a hatchet in the woods. One story claims you can see his ghost in the area above the road in front if where he lived. Later, a woman who lived on the same property had her two year old get electrocuted. Is the place cursed?

Pitts Road: There is a house on Pitts Road where a widow died. On some nights you can see her standing in the window, watching everyone as they go by. If she gets particularly agitated she will fly through the window and chase people, mostly men.

Racetrack Road: A house on Racetrack (sometimes called "Cloverfield", other times called "Windwood Cottage) is supposed to be haunted by several entities. Some of these have been captured on film and EVPs.

Haunted Estill County

The Bells of South Irvine

Riding a bicycle through South Irvine and on toward McKee might not sound like such a good idea these days, what with the multiple vehicles and winding roads. That road wasn't always as crowded with cars, though, and was once a simple lane that saw more horses and farm animals than it did people.

In the early 1900s, a young woman gave birth to a little boy. He was sickly, however, and no amount of home remedies, cuddling, and rocking could pacify him. The young woman, who was often home alone while her husband worked, was tired and exhausted with little sleep and no help. After several months of her baby's crankiness, she was finally able to find someone in town who thought they could make a poultice for him that might help.

It was early in the morning when she started out on her bicycle. Leaving her baby with a neighbor, she sped down the road and toward South Irvine which, at that time, was a thriving community. She probably enjoyed having those moments to herself and looked forward to trying something new in hopes of helping her baby find some peace.

She ended up spending several hours in town, however, by the time she ran her errands and visited with friends whom she hadn't seen in months. It was afternoon by the time she started back and she had underestimated how much the day would take out of her.

Less than a mile from home, she found herself nodding off on her bicycle. Unfortunately, one of the few vehicles on the road chose that moment to round the curve on the wrong side. The car struck her bicycle

Haunted Estill County

and she flew off into the ditch, dying almost on impact.

Today, in the curve, you can sometimes still hear the screech of the car and the bell ringing on her bicycle as the metals clash.

Folk Superstitions

The following is a list of some folk superstitions I've gathered. These were all common beliefs in our part of the state at one time or another. You may have heard your grandparents or parents mention them!

Bees:

Did your grandmother ever tell you that when someone died, you should tell their bees what's going on and cover the hives with a black cloth or ribbon? Some people believe that bees can understand what we say to them and even understand our emotions. For that reason, you might have heard your grandparents talking to the bees and even telling them about what's going on in their lives. In the old days, when a person died, it was thought that someone should inform the bees of their caretaker's death (one of the reasons why a black cloth or ribbon was draped across the hives). If they don't know what's going on, they might fly away.

Salt:

Do you know why it's not a good idea to spill salt? In Ancient Greece and Rome, salt was used for some of the religious ceremonies and was considered blessed. Today, it's still considered important and is often used in Holy water. In the portrait of the last Supper, da Vinici portrays Judas Iscariot spilling salt. As a result, this is considered to be an act of the devil and is a symbol of deceit and lying. During Medieval times some people believed the Devil stood over a person's left shoulder, just waiting to cause mischief. This is why, when we spill salt, we throw it over our left shoulders-in order to try to hit the devil in the face in hopes that he will go away.

Mirrors:

Breaking a mirror is supposed to bring 7 years of bad luck…but why? This goes back to the Roman time when they thought life renewed itself every 7 years. Therefore, if a mirror broke, there would be harm to the person's soul who was last seen reflected in it.

Clocks:

People used to believe that when someone died in the house, the clocks must be stopped at their time of death. If they weren't, then the spirit would stay inside the house.

Hair:

Haunted Estill County

After you had your hair cut, you were supposed to bury it. If you didn't it, the birds might pick it up and then you'd have a headache for a long time.

Superstitions:

If you want to keep a witch out of your house, lay a broom across the doorstep.

A snakeskin bag with a toad's eye inside will ward off ghosts.

A horseshoe hung over the door keeps witches and evil spirits away.

Red sky at sunrise means rain within twenty-four hours.

If you tell a bad dream before breakfast it will come true.

Haunted Estill County

If a bird flies into a house it is a sign there will be a death in the family in the near future.

A cricket in the house brings good luck.

It's bad luck to put a hat on a bed.

If your left ear itches, someone is speaking ill of you.

If the bottom of your right foot itches, you are going to take a trip.

Knock three times on wood after mentioning good fortune so evil spirits won't ruin it.

To get rid of warts, steal someone's dishcloth

Haunted Estill County

and bury it, the warts will disappear.

When you comb your hair, you must not let a bird steal a strand for its nest or you will have headaches all summer.

Never let a swing stop on its own. Stop it yourself or there will be bad luck.

Acknowledgements

As someone not from the county, I occasionally had trouble finding the locations where some of these stories took place. Whenever I heard a new tale, I immediately wanted to set out and find the location. Laken Harris was better than any GPS system I could have used. She was extremely helpful when it came to finding locations for this book and pointed me in the right direction more than once.

I would also like to thank the people who sent me their stories on some of the social media sites and those who shared their ghost stories in restaurants, grocery stories, and hair salons in town. If you were the one of the ones who found themselves telling me about your house/cemetery/former school then I appreciated the time you took to talk to me.

The Estill County Historical Society was good at

answering my questions, pulling up pictures from their archives, and dragging out the maps when I needed them. I always looked at this book as part history/part ghost story so getting the background information on some stories whenever possible was important to me.

Another thank you to the homeowners and residents who let me traipse across their fields and through their farms with my camera.

Special thanks to the following people: Tammy Rose, Tiffany Rose, Joette Morris Gates, and the parents of my son's kindergarten class who helped me connect some of the dots together for many of these stories.

References

Most of the previous stories were told to me by firsthand accounts and are therefore considered a part of oral history. There were some stories, however, that could be corroborated with research.

Irvine: A Hotbed for UFO Activity

"Big UFO Blitz in Kentucky's Baffling Bluegrass Triangle." *National Enquirer*. 1978.

Holland, Jeffrey Scott. "UFO Blitz in the Bluegrass Triangle." *Unusual Kentucky*. March 30, 2011. <http://unusualkentucky.blogspot.com/2011/03/ufo-blitz-in-bluegrass-triangle.html >

Haunted Estill County

"UFO Sightings Report." *MUFON*. Case number 73378. <https://www.sightingsreport.com/sightings/73378>

The Case of the Mysterious Government Agent

"Suicide likely in agent's death." *Kentucky New Era*. October 4, 1990.

Mead, Eileen. "Local man's death ruled suicide." *The Free Lance Star*. October 4, 1990.

"Secret Service agent's stolen Jeep found." *Daily News*. October 9, 1990.

The Haunting of Barnes Mountain

Sources include *The Richmond Climax, The Stanford Interior Journal, The Berea Citizen, The Clay City Times*, and *The Mount Vernon Signal*; all from 1905.

Haunted Estill County
Unsolved Murders

Barnes, Ralph. "Unsolved Murders." *Estill County History*. <http://www.fewpb.net/~ralphbarnes/articles.htm>

The US Gen Web Archives site has a list of important newspaper events for Estill County for the years 1928-1936 at http://files.usgwarchives.net/ky/estill/news/ This site was helpful in putting stories in chronological order and comparing them to others I had heard from members of the community.

The details of Loretta Willoughby's case have been mostly been picked up from stories as told to me by the community. The Kentucky State Police have her murder listed as a cold case on their website at http://www.kentuckystatepolice.org/cold_case/post7coldcase11.php

Sulzer, Elmer G. *Ghost Railroads of Kentucky*. Bloomington, Indiana. Indiana University Press, 1968.

"Southern Lynchings." *Kentucky Genealogy Trails.* 2013. <http://genealogytrails.com/ken/ky_southernlynchings.html>

The Furnaces

"Historic Sites." *Estill County Development Alliance.* <http://www.estillcountyky.net/index.php/play/historic-sites/>

"The Furnaces of Estill County." *Combs' family's website.* <http://echandgs0.tripod.com/combs/index.html>

"Fitchburg Furnace: Past Achievements and Future Goals." *USDA Forest Services.* <http://www.fs.usda.gov/Internet/FSE_DOCUMENTS/stelprdb5282334.pdf>

Haunted Estill County

Barnes, Ralph. "A History of Estill County." <http://www.fewpb.net/~ralphbarnes/estillhist.htm>

Kleber, John E. *The Kentucky Encyclopedia*. Lexington, Kentucky. University of Kentucky Press. 1992.

The Drowning Creek Ambush

This little known story was found during my research after someone told me about soldiers they'd seen on a farm they were exploring. I later found accounts of the story on several genealogy websites. The Estill County Historical Society and the Madison County Historical Society were helpful in trying to help me determine where the incident took place. Dr. Bill Wise of Estill County deserves a particular gratitude for remembering the story being told to him by someone whose grandfather was there and being able to give me the location of the hollow where it took place.

Haunted Estill County

The Devil's House

Robran, Steve. "Devil Worship rumors rampant in portions of Eastern Kentucky." *Kentucky New Era*. September 12, 1988.

"Devil rumors lead to flight for life." *Kentucky New Era*. September 30, 1988.

"Fears of devil worship drive woman from town." *The Telegraph*. October 5, 1988.

Haunted Estill County

Check out other books by Rebecca Patrick-Howard:

More Tales from Haunted Estill County

Windwood Farm

Coping with Grief: The Anti-Guide to Infant Loss

www.ingramcontent.com/pod-product-compliance
Lightning Source LLC
Chambersburg PA
CBHW061322040426
42444CB00011B/2732